# GOD?
# DAMN

*A series of miraculous events that guided the lives*

*of a progressive woman and her daughters*

# CEEJAE DEVINE

Published by Haupthouse Publishing

Haupthouse Publishing, P.O. Box 1811, Lynnwood, WA 98046 U.S.A.

First published in the United States of America

by Haupthouse Publishing, 2023

Paperbound edition published 2023

ISBN: 9798394951121

623-09122023

# GOD? DAMN

Carl Jung said, "I do not need to believe in God; I know. Which does not mean: I do know a certain God (Zeus, Yahweh, Allah, the Trinitarian God, etc.) but rather: I do know that I am obviously confronted with a factor unknown in itself, which I call 'God.'

It is an apt name given to all overpowering emotions in my own psychical system subduing my conscious will and usurping control over myself. This is the name by which I designate all things which cross my path violently and recklessly, all things which upset my subjective views, plans, and intentions and change the course of my life for better or worse. In accordance with tradition, I call the power of fate in this positive as well as negative aspect, and inasmuch as its origin is beyond my control. "god," a "personal god," since my fate means very much myself, particularly when it approaches me in the form of conscience as a Vox Dei, with which I can even converse and argue."

~ An abridged version of Jung's letter to *The Listener*, a BBC Broadcast, January 21, 1960.

# TABLE OF CONTENTS

# ~ S I N G U L A R I T Y ~

1) the state, fact, or quality of being singular

2) something distinguishing a person or thing from others

ALSO:

3) something remarkable or unusual

~ Dictionary.com

# CHAPTER ONE | THE STONE

I REMEMBER THE MINDSPACE OF SINGULARITY.

I can't remember how many times I said, "That isn't fair." One day my father said, "Life isn't fair."

I believed him.

I no longer think anyone should.

## ~THE TOTEM~

We were headed to the most beautiful place in the Pacific Northwest. The Cummins diesel hummed, the boom swayed and creaked as we cruised through an inner passage of the pristine Salish Sea. Randy sat at the helm of our 36-foot Catalina talking to Ken who relaxed with a beer in the stern perch seat. The Sawyer's kids, Jason and Bethany, chattered incessantly as they looked for orcas and eagles. Jade, the youngest member of the crew, followed their lead.

I caught Vicki's eye for a second, but knew she wouldn't try to wade through the verbal fray. Few women did. Most of them sat silent as the guy's conversations skipped across the surface around them. I glanced at Randy. His hair was wild. Spaghetti strands flying out of the tie as Ken joked about his bald-headed good fortune.

The sun was out, but that didn't mean it was warm. I'd learned long before, that even with sunshine from sunup to sundown, my suntan rarely included more than my face and hands.

A barren rock wall, Waldron Island's east side, was on our left. Point Doughty, on the north end of Orcas Island's densely timbered coastline, was coming up on our right. Our destination, the 300-foot-high finger that formed the south side of Fossil Bay on Sucia Island, had separated itself distinctly from the horizon. "See that cliff?" I said, pointing. Jade stood up. I took her hand as she crawled onto one of the cockpit benches. "We'll be on that beach tomorrow."

The kids' attention turned to our fossil hunting expedition. Finding the biggest fossil ever.

The first time Randy and I visited Sucia, he told me that it was okay to take fossils if you didn't dig them out of the cliff. He said they were being destroyed anyway, crushed beneath people's footsteps. I'd collected rocks and shells all my life, from the shoreline of the river behind our home to the shore and rock formations along the Oregon Coast.

I also knew businesses used materials they found in nature. When I was a child, my parents built an addition on our home's river view side. The fireplace, built with chalky white stones embedded with thousands of fractured fossils, was my favorite part. There was also an abandoned quarry site in Sucia's own Fossil Bay. I had no idea when that occurred. All I knew was that lots of people had taken rocks, including fossils, from this area as well as others.

I guided Jade back down to the center of the cockpit, then sat down on the seat under the dodger to get out of the wind. It was Memorial Day weekend. I wanted it to be special for everyone, so I said, "I have a couple of really nice ones. If I find anything tomorrow, you guys can have 'em."

More words flowed unexpectedly. I added, "Unless it's small and special." As I said the last three words, they thundered inside my head.

I sat there in a state of confusion. Stunned.

The conversation around me continued as I tried to process what had just happened. Questions, arguments, and denials erupted.

*What the hell was that?*

I could hear talking, but I couldn't focus on anything around me.

*How did that happen? It has to mean something.*

*No…no. It was just weird.*

*Should I tell everyone?*

*No. They'll think you're crazy.*

We passed Point Doughty, and Randy changed course to head northeast toward Ev Henry Point. Mount Baker came into view.

*Everything seems normal. I haven't lost my mind. Was that God?*

*You're being stupid.*

When we reached the entrance to Fossil Bay, conversations shifted to the preparations we needed to make. The guys sighted a spot on the dock. Somehow I managed to operate on automatic. I got up and headed below to prepare food for the hungry crew. Vicki followed.

Once the boat was secure, Randy put steaks on the grill. I put garlic bread in the oven, got out utensils and plates, and fixed drinks while Vicki made a salad. When everyone was finished, she brought up homemade brownies. As they passed by, I declined. I couldn't tolerate sugar anymore, but I savored a whiff in the breeze.

Ken helped with the dishes while Randy and Vicki watched the kids stretch their legs on the dock for a few minutes. They wanted to go to the beach, but it had been a long day for the Sawyers.

Given the cramped quarters, the Sawyers got ready for bed first. Brushing teeth. Unrolling bedding in the berth under the cockpit. Synchronizing alarms.

I brushed the snarls out of Jade's brown, baby waves, then pulled my hair out the ponytail I'd worn since she started grabbing it with her perpetually sticky hands. I went up on deck to brush it out, closing the companionway doors behind me. The sky was jewel blue. Stars sparkled here and there. I could hear voices from other boats in the bay. Muffled, as if they were far away.

I had been sailing/boating for over ten years, but it was a love/hate relationship. If I could get to the island any other way, I would have. I dreamed about getting a Grand Banks trawler, but for the same size boat, it cost twice as much.

I refused to count how many times a day I ran up and down the companionway steps. Sitting anywhere, inside or out, reminded me of jumping into a pile of leaves. You had to act like it was comfortable, but it wouldn't take long before you realized your butt was numb. Then there were the mosquitos.

I went back inside hoping none had gotten in. Jade and I climbed into the v-berth, and I listened. I could hear them anywhere, and I wouldn't be able to sleep until I found each one. Randy dropped the table in the salon, then came in to give me a kiss and say goodnight to Jade. Once he had settled in, I listened for the maddening buzz, hoping I wouldn't have to get up, but the next thing I heard was Randy talking to Ken in the cockpit.

~ ~ ~

I was usually the last one up. When we had company, which Randy made sure we had more often than not, I always felt like I was being inconsiderate.

Then I had to put on makeup. I envied women who didn't, who were comfortable with their appearance. Vicki was one of them. She looked like someone you'd see in church—clear skin, delicate bone structure, proper.

After breakfast we packed snacks for the kids. Juice and granola bars. Everyone disembarked while Randy secured the cockpit doors. The tide was low, so the ramp was steep. I held Jade's hand until we set foot on land, then I realized even that was going to be challenging. Most of the trails were fine, densely packed soil, but rocks often jutted out and the roots of Douglas Firs, Madrones, and wind-battered Oaks caught toes. The big kids ran ahead, and Jade wanted to keep up with them, so instead, I held my breath.

We crossed the isthmus that separated Fossil Bay from Fox Cove. A place with unsurpassable sunsets framed by sea-sculpted sandstone. As we approached the south side of Sucia, I could see Orcas Island and the place where the weird mind thing happened.

*Am I going to find something?*

*No. You're being an idiot. Forget about it.*

A moderately dry band of stones about the size of a clenched fist ran about halfway between the 300-foot bedrock cliff to our left and the water's edge. It was hard for Jade to navigate, so I held her hand as Jason and Bethany picked up one fossil after another.

"Is this one better? Or this?" they asked.

"I like this one," I said, pointing to a stone Bethany was holding that had a single intact shell rather than the ones with constellations of fragments. "But you have to decide what you like best," I said, as they stuffed them into their pockets. "It looks like you already have too many, and we still have a long way to go. No one is going to carry them for you."

I wanted to stretch my legs at a little faster pace, so about halfway up the peninsula, I asked Randy to watch Jade. We usually went hiking on the island's network of trails, but on this trip, we weren't planning on doing anything else. As I picked up my speed, I wondered how anything unusual could happen. I was speed-walking across a nearly flat uniform expanse.

I stopped about 200 yards from the end of the accessible shoreline and turned to take in the southerly view. I could vaguely distinguish the homes along Orcas Island's North Beach, and because I knew where to look, I could see the stone tower at the top of Mount Constitution.

On the opposite side of the tower, along Orcas' eastern shore, there was a resort with clothes-optional hot tubs. For a couple of years, when Randy and I started to visit the islands, I went, but it was uncomfortable. I spent most of my time trying to convince myself that it wasn't a big deal.

One night we met a guy who had worked with one of Randy's old roommates. After we'd talked for a while, he said, "I've been in your house." It was one of those curious small-world things, and Randy added another friend to his ever-expanding list. On another occasion, a woman said she came to Orcas because it's located on an intersection of high energy lines that circle the planet. She was standing at the far side of the hottest tub, so I didn't have to respond, but I nodded along. I didn't want anyone to see that I thought it was ridiculous.

As I stood on the beach, even though what happened the day before seemed like a surge of energy, my opinion hadn't changed.

I scanned the view again, then looked back at the crew thinking, *See? Nothing is going to happen. That's enough.*

As I turned to join them, I glanced at the ground. A pale streak, like splattered paint, stood out in the field of gray.

I was ninety-nine percent sure I knew what it was, and as I crouched down to pick it up, a chill ran through me. It was a small, egg-shaped rock positioned just right to expose a fossilized crab claw.

I yelled, "Come here! Look what I found!"

Everyone came running, and we took turns examining it. The embedded shell with its distinct, reddish-brown speckling was unmistakable. I stood there wondering if anyone would remember what I said the day before. Then I heard someone say, "It's small." Another said, "And it is really special."

But there was so much more. The fossil held a depth of meaning for me that was at once heartwarming, yet heartbreaking. Mystical, yet I knew for many people, would be laughable. Personal, and even though I thought I'd never use the word, somehow....

*Shit*, I thought. *I'm not going to use it. I hate this. I want to use it, and I can't. The Christian church has taken control of it, like they've done with so many things. I refuse to give any one of them the idea, the slightest possibility, that this has anything to do with their beliefs. But then, what do I call it? What is it?*

As we walked back to the boat, I retreated into a world of my own, overwhelmed by what I was holding.

CHAPTER ONE | THE STONE

# JADE

THE REST OF THE DAY, AND AS WE MADE OUR WAY HOME, no one said anything about the fossil. I wanted to talk about what I'd experienced so badly. The energy spike, or whatever it was that caused the effect on the words I said Saturday, still seemed to be entangled with me, seeking release.

But I couldn't scream. I wasn't even allowed to whisper, "What if this is a talisman? Cancer the Crab is my astrological sign." I could hardly make myself believe it. How could I convince anyone else?

Connections, one after the other, spun through time, back to some of my earliest memories and the most special woman in my life.

~ ~ ~

We were nearing the south end of Orcas. Jones Island was in sight. Everyone was hungry. Randy reduced the running speed and raised the cockpit table. Vicki and I fixed communal plates of deli meat, sliced apples, and cheese and brought them up along with paper-towel napkins. Randy pointed toward the north bay of Jones, "Too bad you guys can't stay a couple more days. There's space on the dock." He turned to the kids and said, "The deer'll eat right out of your hands. Oh yeah, there's Prickly Pear cactus. Great for snacks."

## ~ M I N D S P A C E . 8 ~

I grew up in a desert. One without cactus. The only wildlife: homely house sparrows. It was more like a western stage setup. A fake front.

I didn't know what I was missing until I was about eight years old. One day, I heard my mother talking to a neighbor about a brochure she had seen in New York, before she and my father moved to the west coast. She said she was excited to see that Washington was "The Evergreen State." Then my mother said, "Instead, I found myself in a desert." She must have mentioned Seattle, because I began to dream about going. Then one day we were on our way.

It was already warm, so it must have been early summer. My father's mother, her sister (Aunt Bernice), my parents, and my three sisters piled into our nine-passenger station wagon. Whenever we went on trips my mother always brought Life Savers®. My sisters and I clamored for them immediately. When the package reached me in the far back seat, I carefully pulled away just enough of the paper so I could slide one of my favorites out sideways.

Not long afterwards, we passed through the expanse of sagebrush outside of town. As my Lifesaver disappeared, I started to see greening of the hills. But after we crossed the Vernita Bridge, the highway turned to parallel the Columbia River, so the landscape looked a lot like our back yard. Then, just before Vantage, as we passed by the Sentinel Bluffs, everyone ooh'd and aah'd over the gray basalt rock formations. I couldn't understand why anyone cared. I collected rocks, and they didn't compare.

We climbed the ten-mile hill on the west side of the river, and it felt like I'd entered another world. Ponderosa pines began to dot the hillsides. Through Ellensburg and Cle Elum, sparkling streams broke around rock mounds, wild grasses, and saplings. We travelled up the east side of the Cascades, then over Snoqualmie Pass where we were surrounded by mountains of evergreens. On the west side of the pass, as we made our way through Issaquah, then to Mercer Island, massive bodies of water seemed to appear around every corner. Skyscrapers marked our destination. I watched as they grew, then surrounded us.

The day after we got settled into our hotel in downtown Seattle, we headed to the waterfront and had lunch along the piers. Aunt Bernice ordered a seafood platter, and I had my first taste of Dungeness crab. Salt air drifted through the restaurant. I breathed it in deeply, trying to figure out what I was experiencing. Maybe I assumed it was the same for everyone, so I didn't say anything. But I knew one thing for certain. I loved Seattle. It felt like I had come home to a place I'd never known.

Now Dungeness crab scuttled around in the shallows outside of our community marina and in other bays and shoals in the local archipelago.

## ~ H O M E ~

We approached the marina from the east side to avoid the anchored boats and crab pot buoys. The west side was protected by a man-made breakwater and the east, a rocky outcrop. Randy motored slowly through the entrance and headed to our slip. It was calm. Docking was easy. The Sawyers offloaded first since they needed to catch the ferry, then I went below and began to haul up our stuff.

"Are we going to the ferry?" Jade asked as I set a couple bags on the dockside deck.

Randy grabbed them and headed up to the truck.

"It may be a long wait, so we're going home," I said, grabbing the rest of our bags. We walked up the narrow wooden dock, and I tossed them into the bed. "You know I need to take care of Kiroc and Rocket."

"I wish I could see them again," Jason said, looking up toward the property, running his fingers through curly, blonde tangles.

"We need to get in line," Ken said. "We're pushing it for the 3:15. We'll get home super late if we miss it."

Vicki and Bethany hopped into their suburban. Jason crawled in next to Bethany and closed the door behind him as Ken and Randy made one more trip to haul up their cooler. When they got back, we said our goodbyes. The Sawyers weren't close like family. There were no expectations of hugs, just the usual, "Thank you! Great to see you! Hope we can do it again soon!" They drove out of the gravel parking lot and turned left toward the ferry terminal.

Randy went back to the boat to secure it, then we hopped into the truck and turned right. A few rails of the meadow fence were askew. I wondered if it had been kids or deer passing through. We pulled into the dirt road entrance to the community property and took a hard left into our driveway. Randy drove up to the wooden walkway that wound down to the front door. He built the s-curved, sloping ramp because his ninety-year-old grandfather had driven up from California when Jade was born, and he couldn't navigate stairs. It had been four years, and there still weren't any railings. I constantly worried that someone was going to fall off, especially when it was icy.

Randy ran a load into the house, then went into his shop while Jade and I hauled in the rest.

"We're home! I'll get you out in a minute," I called out to Kiroc and Rocket.

I put my bag in the master bedroom, then put the perishables in the fridge. I went over to Kiroc's cage and unscrewed the clamp that secured the door. She stepped onto my fist, and I ruffled the turquoise feathers around her neck. I could never get enough of her delicate fragrance. Like fresh rainfall, but sweeter. I walked her out to the back deck, set her on her freestanding perch, and attached a tether to the ring on her left leg. I got Rocket out and put him on the perch next to hers. "When are you going to stop plucking your feathers?" I said as he gave me kisses with his soft black tongue.

Jade stood next to the living room table pushing around some plastic beads. I hated moments like this. Our friends were gone. I had chores and work, and Jade was going to be left alone. I tried not to worry. We had just spent a day and a half with non-stop activity.

"You gonna watch a movie?"

Jade nodded.

"Which one?"

"FernGulley."

Jade had figured out how to operate the video machine. I had no idea if that was normal at four.

"You hungry?" I walked into the kitchen to grab a glass of water.

"No."

"Want some water?"

"Kay."

As I filled a glass for me and a cup for her, she put the video in, turned it on, and climbed onto the couch.

I handed her the cup then checked on the birds. They seemed happy enough, so I headed down the stairwell behind their cages. "I'm going to check my messages. I'll be back up in a few minutes."

I scanned my email. A couple of small projects. Then I scanned the emails for Randy's business. Nothing urgent.

I dashed off a draft of the story—without mentioning the weird mind thing—then emailed it to my sisters and a couple of friends. I expected positive responses, but hated knowing I couldn't share the whole story. Then I headed back upstairs to fix dinner.

~ ~ ~

The next day, after I dropped off Jade at preschool, I heated water for my peppermint tea and shuffled through the stack of bills sitting on the practically useless new counter that ran the length the east side of the kitchen. Randy pushed out the wall to increase the kitchen's size, and he installed a full-length skylight flat, so it was speckled with leaves, pine needles, and dirt.

I heard Randy coming down the walkway. I grabbed my cup out of the microwave and dropped in the tea bag, wrapping the string around the handle.

Randy stomped his feet on the doormat and came into the kitchen. He went over to the bills spread out on the counter and flipped through them. "You're not earning enough to pay your bills."

"I should have more work in a couple of days."

"We can't go on like this."

"I don't know where to look."

Randy shook his head, "There's lots of work in Seattle." He opened the fridge, grabbed a can of pop, then headed toward the door. "I'll be at Todd's."

Randy wanted me to look for work every time I had a moment to spare, but it was so hard to do it from the island. It was hard for me to do anywhere. I hated making cold calls. I'd never had much confidence in my creative abilities, but somehow, I had managed to maintain the business for nearly a decade.

I went downstairs to work on the projects that had come in until it was time to pick up Jade.

~ M I N D S P A C E . 3 2 ~

About a year before we moved to the island, I was sure I was going to have to take a full-time job. I had been out of work most of the fall, so I had talked to a few people.

In late December, when we got home from a trip to see my family, there was a light blinking on my answering machine. One of my clients left a message to call another business about a work opportunity. I recognized the address. I'd actually worked in the building a couple of years before. I was pretty sure I knew who the client was, but not a hundred percent. I tried calling the next morning, but reached voicemail, which didn't give me the business' name, so I looked up the address. I was right. Within a few minutes I had an interview for a contract with a major league sports team.

I got the three-month, twenty-hour per week contract to purchase equipment to set up their desktop publishing system, as well as to produce their first in-house magazine and newsletter. It was an incredible addition to my portfolio. It felt like a miracle, but I didn't like using the word. Instead, I told people how lucky I'd been.

Not long after that Randy told me we needed to move because insurance wouldn't cover his new business in the garage. He had been laid off during a period where it was happening to a lot of middle managers or so Randy said. We looked at places from Mount Vernon to Sequim. During that time, a number of my clients called about new and recurring projects, and a couple more referrals came.

~ ~ ~

One weekend, when Randy took a trip to Canada to try to sell some of his merchandise, he took a detour on his way home and went house hunting on Orcas Island. When he told me what he found, I said, "Absolutely not." I wanted to reduce our bills and live credit-free.

Then he explained that the marina at the base of the meadow had a reduced rate, and we could take out an extended loan, so our payments would be comparable to what we had on our current home. When we traveled to look at it together a week later, it felt like a dream come true. For years as we sailed around the island, I'd looked at the homes poised at the far ends of lush green lawns surrounded by evergreens, and I wanted to live there. A couple of months later, we did.

~ ~ ~

Immediately after we signed for the house, the owners took us over to meet Todd and Maya who lived at the far end of the lane. For a while we saw them constantly, but I was overwhelmed trying to adjust to working from the island, which meant taking regular trips to Seattle. It became even harder after Jade was born. I was often trying to manage on four to five hours of sleep while taking one to two trips every week.

One day Randy told me he had seen Maya in the Post Office. He said she told him "I should take the stick out of my ass and be more social." I couldn't believe anyone could say something like that when she didn't have any idea what I was doing.

It had been months since I'd seen her.

## ~ F O U R ~

I turned right onto Killabrew Lane to pick up Jade. There wasn't anyone in sight. I rounded the bend past the ferry terminal and headed up Oofda Hill. Most of the property on the island was composed of large tracts of land. Some of them had ancient Ozlandian orchards that obstructed homes. On others you couldn't see the houses at all. Before we moved, I'd dreamed of finding a community. I had heard that lots of artists lived in the islands including the cartoonist, Gary Larson, and ski film mogul, Warren Miller.

I turned right at Nordstrom Lane, then, just past the recycling station, I slowed down as I passed a couple of deer partially camouflaged in shoulder-high grass. A few minutes later I came to the intersection that led to the west side of the island. Horseshoe Highway veered to the right into Eastsound. A few blocks up, another left, then I turned into the pre-school parking lot.

I jumped out of the truck and walked around the front of the little blue and white cottage to the back yard where I knew I would find Jade. She was playing in the sandbox as I approached.

"Time to go home," I said.

She didn't respond. She just got up and wiped off her hands. We walked into the house to collect her belongings. As we passed by Sonya, one of the preschool teachers, she said, "Jade hasn't been her usual sparkly self this afternoon. She might not be feeling well."

"Thanks," I replied. "I'll call you tomorrow if she's not feeling better."

I helped Jade into the truck and put my hand on her head. "You don't have a temperature. Are you hungry?"

"No."

"You sure?"

I climbed in the driver's side and backed out. As we headed back down Horseshoe Highway, Jade stared at her hands. Something wasn't right.

"Did something happen today?"

"I guess so."

"What?"

"One of the boys yelled at me."

"What did he say?"

Jade didn't respond.

I could see she was struggling. "I can't help if I don't know what he said." I thought, *Maybe she doesn't know how to explain it.*

She looked down again, then back at me, "He screamed at me, 'Fuck you! Fuck you! Fuck you!'"

She was four.

"Oh my God. I'm sorry sweetie. I'll tell your father. Who was it?"

"Justin."

He came over from the elementary school after classes ended for the day. A second or third grader.

"Okay. It was important for you to tell me. Your father and I will get this straightened out."

## ~ M I N D S P A C E . 1 8 ~

There are some things in life that shake you. They come out of nowhere and you do your best to cope.

But one time, shortly after I arrived in Seattle with my best friend, Liz, I felt like I'd gotten a hint. For years I wondered how it affected my decisions, my path.

We were heading to the Seattle Center. I hadn't seen the city since I'd visited with my family. I was getting impatient as Liz sat on the floor slowly turning one of her socks inside out, at least that's how it seemed. Then she started to fuss with the other one.

"Do you really need to do that?" I asked.

I was ready to go, standing there thinking, *Why does anyone need to turn their socks inside out?*

We finally pulled out of the parking lot in her red Camaro, turning left onto Highway 99, then left again onto I-5. As we came around a curve in Tukwila, I could see the skyscrapers on the horizon. When we reached the Rainier Building, a couple of guys drove up beside us and started waving. We tried to ignore them, but they kept pace and followed us to the Center.

It didn't seem like a problem until they followed us back to our apartment. Suddenly I found myself alone with one of the guys. Liz had disappeared, and I became disoriented. The guy started telling me about a hangout on Alki

Beach, how you could see the lights of Seattle. I told him I needed to study, but it was Saturday night, and he wouldn't take no for an answer.

I got into his tan sedan, and we headed north on I-5, then we took the exit for the West Seattle Bridge. We stopped at a place that was practically vacant. The gray linoleum floors and white tabletops matched my mood. The guy had a couple of beers while I sipped on one, then we headed out. He turned north, which took us up a hill that curved to the west.

As I was trying to figure out how I was going to avoid making out with him, he calmly informed me, "I'm not Garrett Cantela, I'm Jack the Ripper."

As the words came out of my mouth, I wondered why I was talking at all, but it's all I had. "If you don't have a gun or a knife, I'm going to put up a hell of a fight."

I don't remember anything after that until I was pinned under the steering wheel with his hands around my throat. I tried to beg him to stop, but without any air the sound that came out was a grotesque, distorted groan. I thought, *This is it.*

I had no idea how much time had passed when I suddenly realized I was still alive. I thought, *Did he pass out? What do I do now?*

The guy was lying across my legs. *How do I get up? Is he faking it because he didn't want to kill me?*

The only way I could do anything was to push him off. I couldn't believe he didn't wake up. I looked at the dark, quiet residential neighborhood. There wasn't anyone in sight.

I probably qualified for the "Darwinian Award" for what I did next. The keys were in the ignition, and I started it. I don't know how I found my way back to the main road or to the hill we drove up so I could get back to the freeway, but I drove myself home.

When I got to the apartment, Liz met me at the door. "Oh my God," she said. "What happened? Go look in the mirror."

I told her everything as I looked at my face, my eyes. The blood vessels had burst along the bottom edges.

"You need to call the police."

When they arrived, Garrett was still passed out. There wasn't any question about what happened. They took him away and asked me if I wanted to press charges. I was afraid he would come back and kill me if I did. I submitted a statement with a court clerk, instead, saying that said if he ever assaulted anyone else, I would testify against him.

I didn't know what to call the feeling I had about the time delay as Liz was putting on her socks. All I knew is that it felt like something was wrong. I also knew with absolute certainty that I couldn't tell my parents.

~ ~ ~

I believed most people were good, so it didn't take long for me to find a boyfriend. A short time later, Liz said the situation wasn't working for her, and she made plans to leave.

Did the situation with Garrett scare her? Did it scare her mother enough that she talked Liz into attending a bigger college? Was Liz lonely? Probably. Liz and I didn't ever talk about it.

I called my father and told him. I also told him I wanted to try to find a way to stay. At that moment I knew that keeping the information about what happened with Garrett from my parents had been the right decision.

~ ~ ~

While it seemed like Liz's decision should have thrown my life into turmoil, I stayed focused on the belief I could stay in Seattle.

As I hung up the phone on one call after another to universities that wouldn't take me mid-year, it began to feel like it was going to be impossible. When I finally heard yes, it was still daunting. It was a private school. The cost was significantly higher than what I thought I should ask of my father, but I asked anyway.

~ ~ ~

Over time I began to feel like I could see exactly which personality traits my mother and father had given to each one of their daughters, as though they handed them out to us as gifts.

Mother: "I need noise in my environment all the time. You'll thrive in silence."

Father: "You will get my love for the city. I'll do anything to support you because I know you'll be living there forever. I'm giving you my dream."

~ ~ ~

I knew the private school would take anyone that had the money, still, it felt like a miracle that I managed to stay in Seattle.

I wanted to transform myself so people would see me as the oasis that surrounded me. Like I belonged in a place with stately red-brick buildings and a neatly manicured campus that was a hop, skip, and jump to Broadway, home to lots of creative, free-spirited people.

One day on campus, however, I saw the reflection of the burden I carried reflected in the eyes of a girl I'd known in high school, *What's a girl like you doing in a nice place like this?*

I didn't know what was normal, but I knew I didn't fit the description. I was comfortable being alone. I was willing to try almost anything. I wanted to be loved, but I had difficulty communicating verbally. I also wanted to know more about God after reading a book I knew wouldn't be accepted in the

Catholic or Lutheran churches my family attended off and on up until I was about ten.

My mother always had a collection of books. She seemed to practically disappear in them. One day she left *The Source* by James A. Michener on a table in the living room.

Michener took me back to the time when people were beginning to develop ideas about God. He followed the lineage of various members of one community up until the present day, showing how their beliefs, and the beliefs of others, influenced their lives.

Michener introduced a woman called Gomer. I couldn't think of a name I hated more. I grew up watching Jim Nabors as Gomer Pyle, a naïve, incompetent guy. The woman in Michener's book was completely different. She started to think she was hearing God's voice, and over time, God spoke through her. It had never occurred to me that something like that could happen to a woman.

But it was fiction. No one was supposed to believe it.

~ ~ ~

Even though the university was Jesuit, students weren't required to take courses in religion. But one afternoon, God showed up in my Philosophy course. (I'm sure it's no surprise to anyone that they would find some way to include it.)

The professor was talking about the Big Bang theory that was initially proposed in 1927 by Georges Lemaître, a professor of physics at the Catholic University of Louvain. The philosophy professor said, "How could order come from chaos? The universe is filled with structural order: growth patterns of crystals, logarithmic spirals of nautilus shells, a butterfly's bilateral symmetry. Science isn't necessarily antithetical to creation theories."

I thought, *Finally, proof that God exists.* I could cross that question off my list.

~ ~ ~

Not that I expected it to change anything. I was going to be an engineer. I managed to get a decent grade in Algebra at the community college, and I thought that would be enough to propel me forward. Liz was taking engineering courses, and if she could do it, I could, too.

The only other things that held any sort of interest to me were English and Art. Somehow I knew no one could get a decent paying job in either.

Still, art was like an extra lifeline that had grown from my heart. Instead of having three main arteries supplying me with the life force, it was as if I had a fourth: the artofme.

## ~MINDSPACE.9~

When Aunt Bernice moved from the East Coast to live with Gramma, she shared her love of arts and crafts with me and my big sister, Valerie.

After sitting at her large wooden dining room table sipping tea with two, and only two, sugar cubes, we walked along the dike about a block from her house and collected wildflowers. When we got back, we pressed them in books, and, later, put them in decorative frames. We also crafted various kinds of holiday decorations.

Then she died when I was nine.

I continued to work on art projects, but failed in some way every time. I couldn't help but compare my work to Valerie's. As a child, I wasn't able to consider the fact that she was three years older. Valerie started a rug hooking, so I did, too—a three-foot Dungeness crab.

It didn't take long for it to find its way into a closet, then into the trash, because the burlap had pulled away from the frame.

Still, I kept trying. At one point, I created a clay pot with a bird on top.

The wings hung over the edges and were broken off in the firing process. In high school I was using stick figures for a screen-printing project, while one of my classmates was creating an illustration for a local business.

My creativity was a sad, scrappy thing, but everything else I tried was worse.

Aunt Bernice was also the only person outside of church who shared anything with me about their beliefs. When Valerie and I stayed overnight, she would bring out a bottle of holy water, draw a cross on my forehead, and say, "Goodnight, sleep tight to wake up bright in the morning light to do what's right."

With everything the kids did in the neighborhood and everything I saw at home, it was hard to know what was right before Aunt Bernice died, and even harder after she was gone.

## ~MINDSPACE.20~

The university allowed me to express myself freely, to push myself, but also to accept my unique process. For some reason, in that space, I didn't have any fear that anyone was going to criticize me. I still carried the fear that somehow, at some point, I would experience repercussions from the life I was trying to escape, but for short periods of time, that space allowed me to forget about where I'd come from and feel my way through artistic discovery in a way that felt right to me.

Part of that involved creating an image of God that made sense to me. It wasn't something I did consciously, and it took a couple of steps.

~ ~ ~

Winter quarter I took Algebra/Trigonometry, Philosophy, and a drawing course. *For balance*, I thought.

For one of the assignments, I created a red, yellow, and orange geometric face floating in space. It had an androgynous quality. A calm, peaceful gaze. A star that had energy radiating from the mind-space.

During my second year, I took Latin, Chemistry, and Calculus for the first two quarters. I was proud of what I was accomplishing in math, but I slowly began to realize that the other students had foundations I didn't have. They would say, "Just use the 'X' formula," and I had no idea what they meant.

With a little help, I managed to figure out enough, so I signed up for Calculus again spring quarter, but I needed a break. I lightened my load with a course in Psychology and another art course, Graphics.

At the end of the first week, the professor gave us a quiz. I stared at the first question for a minute. It was pulled directly from the text but missing a couple of words. The instructions:

Fill in the blanks. An exact match gets four points, a close match three, a good guess two, and something related, one.

The rest of the questions were similar, until I reached the end.

There was an empty box about two inches square with the instructions: Draw Figure 3.1.

I thought, *This is ridiculous. No one can get an "A" in this class.*

I went to the professor's office one afternoon and complained. He said, "I want you to learn to think differently."

The professor also assigned weekly art projects.

~ ~ ~

For one, we were instructed to use four elements: a printed image, a line, a square, and a point.

I created another face free-floating in space. A more personal version. It was enhanced by a mishap that occurred with the glue. Where the glue bled out from the image, the black marker made the "space" shiny, luminescent, so I covered the entire black area with glue then ran the marker over it again.

The eyes on the face turned downward as if in contemplation with hands crossing below, like a form of protection. This image had more of a feminine presence, still with the serenity of a deity. But it also felt like a self-portrait. The androgynous name, "Jonmarcol," sat along the bottom edge.

~ ~ ~

One day near the end of the quarter, the professor stopped me and said, "You are really creative."

I don't know why I believed him. Maybe it was because I didn't have any other options.

I applied to the Graphic Design program at the University of Washington.

It was competitive. Each fall 100 students were accepted, but only 50 continued the second quarter. At the end of the second quarter, 25 students would finish the year and become the incoming class the next fall.

Somehow, I made it.

## ~ M I N D S P A C E . 2 1 ~

Nearly a year after the professor talked to me about thinking differently, it didn't seem like anything had changed. Sure, I'd figured out how to pass his tests, but my mind still seemed to still be a clunky engine, functional, but frustrating to operate.

Then one afternoon, as I stood outside my dorm in the bright Seattle sunshine, I noticed an incredible sense of mental clarity, as if my mental circuits had been purged of impurities. I thought, *That's different.*

A short time later, I was given an assignment to design a cover for a book about politics. I stopped by the library on my way home and picked up *The Politics of Women's Liberation.* I expected the usual. Hours of mental torment trying to come up with something good enough. But the next day when I was running an errand, waiting for a light on 12th Ave., I had a clear mental picture of a strong design concept. I thought, *What just happened? I wasn't even thinking about it.*

I had no idea that the creative process could work like that. Just pour in some information and let my mind work in background mode while I was doing something else.

But as each quarter progressed, as project after project was completed and presentations were made, it became clear that I wasn't as good as most of the other students. They were like the guys in Calculus. They knew about concepts and techniques I'd never heard of.

I headed to Seattle Art as often as I could, trying to compensate by buying "graphic design Cliff Notes"– magazines like *Communication Arts, Graphis,* and *Print.* On some projects, I spent hours struggling to come up with a design that was just passing compared to the quality of the other students' work. I searched and waited and pushed ideas around, hoping that once again that elusive creative connection to the great problem solver would offer a best-of-class solution. Hoping that all I would have to do is turn my head in the right direction, and I'd see it right behind my eyes.

I constantly wondered, *Why am I here?*

I felt like a graphics groupie, a wannabe, while my classmates were graphics gods that seemed to have a direct connection to a creative force that they could use at will, and I was dialing in and constantly getting a busy signal.

## ~ O N L I E S ~

Randy got back at about 6:00 p.m. He was always on the go. I had stopped asking questions. Randy cast out a net everywhere he went, hauling in one new friend after another. They always had projects to work on – fixing roofs, building greenhouses, adding rooms, adding gadgets to their boats.

I told Randy what happened at preschool and he said he'd take care of it, then he settled into the couch and turned on the TV.

Jade helped me prepare enchiladas, and after dinner, I put the leftovers in the fridge. Cleanup was easy so I didn't bother Randy about it. Jade followed me downstairs as I made my way carefully down with the birds. I put them outside and spent a few minutes with them while giving them room to stretch their wings. After I checked both email accounts and reviewed the work I had for the next couple of days, I read a couple of books to Jade. Then I got out some colored pencils so she could draw while I worked on an editing project.

It didn't take long before it was too hard to concentrate. Things hadn't turned out the way I hoped they would. Instead of finding community, it felt like the vacant space around me had grown exponentially.

There weren't any kids in the neighborhood. No one lived full time in the houses around us. Family was hundreds of miles away, and I wasn't the kind of artist that could mingle with others at local events. For quite a while I'd been thinking about having another child. The house would be filled with a presence that would bring new energy, new dynamics. Not for me or even Randy. For Jade.

I hunkered down and finished the project, then I composed an email and sent it to the client.

~ ~ ~

When Jade and I went back upstairs, Randy was asleep in the crook of the couch. I sat on the end near the fireplace, and Jade curled up on my left. I flipped through TV channels until I found a nature program, then put my feet up on the glass table. It was one of the things I loved most in our home. The base was a tangle of driftwood sculpted from copper with silver-leaf sprays. We found it at a Bellevue art gallery and had side tables built to match. The artist told us it had taken multiple attempts to develop a technique that made the metal look like natural bark.

About an hour later Randy sat up and turned on the news. Jade looked sleepy, so I brushed her teeth and put her to bed. I put a blanket over the bird cages before I joined Randy again.

"I don't think it's fair for Jade to be an only child," I said as I tossed a pillow on the glass tabletop to cushion my feet.

"It takes a quarter million bucks to raise a kid nowadays."

"I'm not saying it won't be hard."

"Yeah? What about my retirement?"

"I don't think I'm ever going to be able to retire."

"Onlies are more successful."

Randy was nine years older, so I didn't expect him to view life the same way I did. Still, I didn't know how anyone made this kind of decision. I was among the first generations of women who, even though we were married, had to make the decision to get pregnant unless it was an accident.

It felt like the evil twin of the "problem that had no name" Betty Friedan described in the 50s where women struggled with feelings about not being in control of their lives. That generation wasn't supposed to want to go to college and have a career. They were supposed to want to stay home with their children.

I wasn't supposed to think there was even a remote possibility that I could quit work to care for my kids. I was supposed to be a happy wife and worker, pooling my funds with my husband's, striving toward our mutual goals, and enthusiastically having sex without having to worry about consequences until "we" decided it was time.

But when was that time? Who was the "we" that said, "Let's have a child."

I went back to the master bathroom to get ready for bed. The old brown countertop and mirror were filthy. I had completely lost interest in housecleaning, but I had come up with a way to keep things tolerable. I called it the "five-minute pickup." It was hard to tell myself I didn't have time for that. After I brushed my teeth, I went back out to the living room to kiss Randy goodnight, then I went down to the spare bedroom at the end of the hallway and climbed in with Jade.

~ ~ ~

Tap, tap, tap….
Tap, tap, tap….
Knock, knock, knock….

I was hoping I could ignore Randy long enough to get him to stop. I was afraid he was going to wake up Jade. We were also on a community well system and our neighbors got angry if anyone used too much water. I waited another minute, but the water kept going. I crawled out of bed and brushed my teeth, calling out, "Be there in a minute."

I climbed into the shower and wet down my hair. I still had the weight I'd gained from breastfeeding Jade, which I did for nearly 18 months. I felt like I had the right to eat whenever I wanted, and I usually ate something before bed. Randy would sit on the couch next to me and talk about having a weight loss contest. I knew he wouldn't do it. It was just his way of telling me I was too fat. I scrubbed my hair, face, and body, turning away from him as often as I could so he couldn't see my bulging tummy.

I wanted another child, but I had completely lost interest in sex. We'd been married twelve years. It wasn't an exaggeration to say we'd done it a thousand times. It probably wasn't an exaggeration to say we'd done it two. And I spent more time than I cared to think about trying to convince Randy we weren't the only ones who weren't at eight. We worked from home. Why wasn't I up for it twice a day?

I dried off and crawled into the master bed. Randy didn't seem to care how I felt about it. Afterwards, we dressed in silence, and I went to the kitchen. Randy yelled from the door as he headed out, "I'm not starting any new projects today. Just leave the P.O.'s on the table."

## ~MINDSPACE.11~

When I was ten or eleven I wanted twelve children. One from every country. That was the extent of my knowledge about geography.

## ~MINDSPACE.26~

I also wanted to get pregnant on our honeymoon, but I was on birth control, so I waited, hoping I could figure out when the time was right. I asked Randy about it on one of our boating trips. We were tied up at the docks in Olympia, and I said, "Do you want children?" He hesitated a moment, but then he said, "Yeah."

I talked to friends and family about it. I wondered about the impact on the environment, if it would be better to adopt. Year after year passed.

One morning on my way to work I felt like I was going to fall asleep at the wheel. I couldn't get off the couch on the weekends. A few days later when I was driving to the mall, I couldn't keep my eyes open. I couldn't remember if

I had locked the bird cages. I stopped to call Randy and left my purse at the gas station.

I still wanted children and thought, *I have to be strong if I'm going to work full time.* I had a history of allergies, so I changed my diet. Then, I went through a series of tests administered by a naturopath physician and was told I was allergic to alcohol. I also stopped taking "The Pill."

## ~ M I N D S P A C E . 3 3 ~

We were in the middle of the decision to move to the island when I realized I was pregnant. I told Randy, "If we don't move now, we'll never make it."

I didn't tell my clients. It seemed like it was enough for them to have to adjust to the move. I would show them there wouldn't be any difference in the kind of service I could offer. Then I would show them I could do the same when the baby came.

The island only had a small medical facility, so I started seeing a midwife. She said, "That's not how it works. You're going to have to be a cow for a while."

I thought, *You've obviously been living on a farm. I'm a city girl. I'll figure it out.*

~ ~ ~

At 6:00 a.m. one morning, I woke up with a backache. It didn't surprise me. I'd spent the entire day before cooking. When Randy left that evening to make a supply run, there were pots and pans everywhere.

The phone rang about 9:00 a.m. Randy was checking in. I told him I was fine and reminded him of my cooking frenzy. He was staying with friends who were like second parents. He told me I should talk to Margery.

"I said I'm fine."

"Here she is."

I told her what I told Randy. She said, "You should call the midwife." I agreed (mostly to end the conversation) and thanked her. Then I decided to call the midwife anyway. She wasn't available so I left a message.

About an hour later she returned my call. I told her Randy wanted me to call, but I thought I was fine. As I said that my voice cracked.

She said, "What are you doing?"

"I'm trying to get comfortable. I'm on the floor. On my hands and knees."

She said, "You're in labor.

~ ~ ~

Six hours later the nurse put Jade on my tummy. I couldn't believe my eyes. I mean her eyes. They were huge, bright, fixed intently on mine. I lay there thinking, *Aren't newborns supposed to be wrinkly red things that have their eyes closed, like puppies?* I loved the sparkly copper color. Like a bracelet I'd worn for years as a teenager.

The midwife told me my life would change when Jade was born, but this was different from anything I imagined. I held on to the moment, the glorious gift of the unexpected.

The next day passed in a blur. Then the following morning I took Jade to her first checkup. When the midwife saw how alert she was, I mentioned that it had been constant.

She said, "We call these babies 'little wizards.'" She tossed the words out casually, as if people said things like that every day.

It sent a chill through me. Then I thought, *It doesn't really* mean *anything, does it?*

## ~ N A T H A N ~

Jade was speaking clearly by the time she was two. At one point a year or so later, as I was standing by Jade in front of the fireplace, she turned to me and said, "I thought my father's name was supposed to be Nathan."

I hadn't said anything to her or Randy about him.

As the seconds passed, I thought, *"Did I really hear that?"*

I was sure I did. I wanted to hold on to the sound of her words, but they quickly faded.

I didn't know what to do but say no. I shook my head and walked away. I couldn't share it with anyone.

I couldn't understand how something like that could happen. Jade knew something that had only existed in my mind, that had never been a reality. Yet she thought it was supposed to be.

There was a connection between us that went beyond what I thought was possible, what was once an intense longing, but that could also be considered nothing more than a thought, resided in both of our minds.

## ~ M I N D S P A C E . 2 5 ~

For close to four years, I lived in a glorious fantasy. Then, when I graduated from college, the guy I had been dating, Nathan, left Seattle. We talked about visiting, and I kept hoping that he loved me, that I would be able to live that dream, but it had become clear, he couldn't spend the rest of his life with someone like me.

I dreamed about staying connected to him forever. I dreamed about having his child, but I knew from experience how awful it was to do that to someone.

In some ways, it felt like Nathan wanted me to know what love could be, but he also knew he wouldn't be able to give me the forever version or at least the forever version most people expected.

Nathan called one last time about two years after we graduated. It was heartbreaking to hear his voice. To tell him I'd gotten married. To let him know I believed I'd found someone who could, who would, actually love me.

Randy was energetic and passionate about work and play. He maintained our yard like an arboretum. I practically worshipped the weeping cedar at the entrance to our driveway.

We cooked together and canned fruit and vegetables in the fall. We skied Whistler, Snoqualmie Pass, and Alpental.

He encouraged me to start my business, but that's where I began to see that we were different. He constantly pressured me to take business clients to lunch.

I tried again and again, but I was always uncomfortable. It was hard to find enough to talk about without having to figure out how to eat in the middle of it. Moments of silence were excruciating. Because Randy managed conversations so easily, I added it to the list of things that were wrong with me.

# AMBER

"REBECCA NEEDS ANOTHER BROCHURE."

"Yeah?"

Randy plunked down on the couch while I got out eggs, cheese, and some leftover crab for omelets. I cracked a bunch of crab, but when I started shredding the cheese, I had to take a break. I crossed my arms in front of me and leaned on the counter.

"I'm going to head down Thursday. It may be the last time I can get down there for a while."

"I'll call Maya. Jade can stay with her."

I cracked two eggs into a bowl, then washed my hands. I stared out the kitchen window at the property below Randy's shop. A grassy, teardrop-shaped empty space. Randy continued to maintain his friendship with Todd and Maya. Jade hadn't seen her for months so it was hard to know how comfortable she would be there. Sometimes Randy ran around the island three times a day. I didn't understand why he couldn't at least take her to preschool, but I didn't want to sound like I was constantly watching him. I finished preparing the omelets, then cut up an avocado and some red peppers.

~ ~ ~

The next morning I dropped Jade off at preschool. When I got home, I took the birds downstairs, setting their perches close enough together that they could move back and forth between them. It was still cool out so I kept them inside, then I went back upstairs to get a cup of tea. The phone rang.

"Ceejae?"

"Hi, yeah. Maryann? How are you?"

"I'm afraid I have some bad news."

"Oh. Okay?"

"You know we recently hired Sharron."

"Yeah?"

"Well, I wanted to see what she could do before I let you know, but she's going to be able to produce the magazine more efficiently. We're going to do it in-house. She should be able to manage everything we need. Of course, we'll keep you in mind if anything changes."

I started shaking, afraid Maryann could hear it in my voice.

"Okay. Sure. It's been nice working with you. Feel free to call anytime."

A $10,000 bi-annual project. Gone.

Maryann was the marketing director for a private school in Seattle. I'd been working with her for almost three years. I hadn't told her I was pregnant. I also hadn't told Randy that I had already been worried about my ability to produce the next edition.

I didn't tell Randy a lot of things. Like spending twice as much time on almost every project than what I charged because I felt like I needed to make sure everything was perfect. But even that didn't eliminate mistakes. When a client was paying hundreds or thousands of dollars and found a mistake on the end product, I wanted out. I wanted to quit, but if I did, even to take a short break, I wouldn't be able to build the business back up again. Not out here, anyway.

~ ~ ~

I left on the redeye Thursday morning and struggled to keep myself from crying. I blasted Led Zeppelin, Fleetwood Mac, and Fresh Aire III as I drove down the freeway in an attempt to power wash away my frustration.

When I reached the development, I wound my way through the broad streets lined with spindly young trees. I was finally able to see some of the finished homes. They had nice features like large sidewalks, front porches, and mixed-use buildings, but to me they didn't compare to the home Randy and I left in Maple Valley and the one we currently lived in.

Rebecca's office was at the Information Center, an open space that featured a gorgeous clock tower. She hadn't changed. She always wore her bleach-blonde hair short and her dark blue suit made her look sharp. I was wearing dress-casual, never feeling like I could pull off the look she seemed to do so easily. She reviewed a packet of photos and the text with me, then offered to take me on a tour.

The focus of the Information Center was a computer that allowed potential buyers to take interactive, virtual tours. Cutting edge technology. Suddenly I felt small, incompetent, as I realized that this was the direction the world was heading and there wasn't any way I could get there.

As we walked the grounds past the houses, I thought about how different our lives were, about how she had given up having children and made her way into upper management. Rebecca was also one of the sweetest people I'd ever met, and that was hard for me. She was so friendly that I could never figure out how to reciprocate. Given the amount of time we had, the conversation turned to our personal lives.

Rebecca shared some of the struggles she had with a man she had married and divorced, wondering if she could ever marry again. We commiserated about how difficult it was to find a good relationship, and I told her I was pregnant again.

"Late July," I said.

"That's wonderful," she replied.

We circled back to the entrance of the cul-de-sac, and I thanked her for showing me around. Everything I did made me feel awkward. I wanted to tell her how much I appreciated her friendship, but I was there for business and didn't want to cross a line.

~ ~ ~

I plowed back up I-5. This time in silence. It was so hard to see that computer system, to know I would never be able to create video animations. Somehow I knew it with absolute certainty, and I didn't know what it was going to do to me.

After about 20 minutes, I passed Commencement Bay. Another 10 minutes and I passed the apartment I'd shared with Liz. It felt like I was driving up a timeline. Past the exit where a man told me he was Jack the Ripper. Past the exit to the YWCA, where I stayed as I waited to attend the Jesuit college.

As I crossed the Ship Canal Bridge, I could see the UW campus and the green, copper clad steeple of the church I attended with Nathan.

His religious beliefs affected his feelings toward me. I wasn't any better. Whenever I thought about my past, I always backtracked just to the point in my early teens when I decided to cross the bridge that led away from religion.

As if I made that decision in a void.

A couple of poetic phrases surfaced that seemed important, that went further back.

The north side of Everett was one of my time markers. If traffic and weather conditions were good, I could make it to the ferry in an hour. I looked at the clock as traffic slowed as I made my way down the ramp perched over the sloughs south of Marysville. 5:17 pm. Catching the 6:35 pm was going to be challenging. Sometimes I had to make the drive in the pouring rain. After getting up at 5:00 a.m., I would often find myself driving home at 75 to 80 mph so I could catch the earliest sailing. One night I realized I could get into an accident. Maybe not even make it home.

I started writing, to Jade.

~ ~ ~

I finally cleared Marysville, then Smokey Point and the exit to Camano Island. Pigeons swooped in close to the truck and tucked into the supports of the overpass to Conway. I passed Cascade Mall and took the next exit, heading west through the Skagit farmlands. I crossed the man-made slough that created Fidalgo Island, and headed on to Anacortes. When I arrived at the terminal, the ferry attendant was flagging cars. Once I got to my parking spot, I decided to walk around the car deck, so I waited until everyone finished loading.

The departure announcement echoed inside the tunnel. I opened the door and stretched. I walked to the back and watched the ferry churn the water into blue marble.

The ferry set its course northwest toward Cypress Island to clear Shannon Point, so it was calm as I climbed the ramp to the upper parking deck then made my way back down to the bow. The sky was a monotone, sleep-inducing blue, so I turned around and made another loop.

The ferry completed its turn and headed west. It was still warm. I walked around a couple more times thinking that it was strange that there wasn't even a breeze in the cavernous space. As I worked my way through the cars, I couldn't decide if I should go up or continue walking. I thought the wind was going to make the decision for me. We were approaching the passage between Decatur and Blakely when it occurred to me that Randy and I hadn't talked about baby names.

I stood on the bow, enjoying a moment of my own. Quiet. Uninterrupted. But the view was uninspiring. The rise of Lopez Island ahead was nondescript. Blakely, a mass of evergreens. Then the name, Amber, came to me.

Aunt Bernice. The baby had to be named after Aunt Bernice. Aunt Bernie. Amber.

Golden. Translucent. Like a jewel but down to earth.

~ ~ ~

I went up to the passenger deck and got out the recycled paper journal I was using to write to Jade. I did and I didn't want to tell her about my life.

The ferry turned north toward Spencer Spit.

~ M I N D S P A C E . 1 3 ~

When I was thirteen or so, I thought I had it all figured out: that you'd better know shit, and you'd better be beautiful.

But, I was told, I needed to be careful about who I listened to or I'd end up in some godforsaken, fiery hot, desolate place. A place you never, ever, wanted to go.

Kind of like the place where I grew up.

What I remember from the first ten years or so smoldered, like remnants of a house burned down. Scorched ground that still burned to the touch.

When I was seven or eight, I was introduced to the forbidden world by a boy in my neighborhood. "If milk ever comes out of a woman's breasts before she gets pregnant, it's poisonous. Touch the dog's balls. I dare ya."

Every day I walked by a nude statue of a woman that sat in the middle of our living room. Dark green with a charcoal sheen. Crouching down on one knee, her hair flowing part-way over her breasts. I felt like I had to find a way to accept her, but every day, I struggled with her presence.

I was left alone in the house. A lot. I had three sisters, but for some reason I was left at home.

Was it after Aunt Bernice died? Had I become a difficult child? Was my mother mad at me? Was it just easier for her to only have to deal with three children when she went shopping? How many times did she go every week to keep enough food in the house for six people? Two? Three?

Somehow, I knew about the *Playboys*.

When I looked through them, I knew I had to keep watch out my parents' bedroom window, which looked out over the driveway. I knew I had to put the magazine back exactly how I found it and get out of their room before anyone came in. I peeked out every so often through the blinds. I listened for the sound of car doors.

The little girl who loved to read. Who was so proud of her ability to advance quickly through the increasingly difficult sets of self-study books in second, third, and fourth grade.

Was I just curious? Did I go around looking through everything just to see what was there? One day a childhood friend went through a medicine cabinet and collected all kinds of pills. Did I learn it from her?

How did I get a copy of *The Happy Hooker* in high school? How did I even know about it? Was I a rebel or the kind of woman the patriarchy wanted?

Women who were silent. Like my mother.

Women who would try to make themselves desirable. Like my mother.

Women who would center their lives around men.

One day I found myself at the end of the hallway where my parent's bedroom started. The bathroom was on the right. The linen closet on the left.

My mother was facing the mirror, topless. She turned her head. Just her head. She didn't say anything, like "Hi, sweetie. Do you need anything?" She just stood there while I tried to figure out how to deal with the discomfort.

It was the first time I can remember her staring at me like that. Each time, from then on, she made me feel like an intruder.

Every time I sifted through the remnants of my childhood, fragments here and there would give a moment's hope that I'd remember happiness, but everything was tinged with blackness.

A realm of vast shadowy spaces.

Events collapsed through time, piling onto one another in juxtapositions and connections that often felt like cruel jokes.

Even my first memory became blighted.

When I was sixteen or so, I went to a grocery store to buy a pack of smokes, and found myself looking into the eyes of the woman from the only memory I had before I was five years old. A brief moment when I was about two. I was watching her paint a jigsaw-cut lamb. Then she gave it to me. It had the sweetest face and huge, irresistible eyes, and at that moment mine were locked with hers as I stood there wondering if she knew who I was.

## ~ P R E P A R A T I O N S ~

When they announced our arrival at Orcas, I hustled down to the truck. As I inhaled the brisk, salt air, I remembered the name, Amber. *Was I just told we were having a girl?*

~ ~ ~

I ran my briefcase down to my office. There was still some daylight, so I put the birds on the deck. Frogs were deep into their evening songs in damp meadow crevices and along the edges of the pond. I grabbed a banana and took it to them. They took turns, although Rocket always took more than he could manage, dropping chunks on the newspaper-liner.

Randy and Jade had already eaten, so I sliced a banana on a plate for myself and grabbed a jar of peanut butter.

"Anything exciting happen today?" I said, as I unscrewed the lid.

"No."

I was wrung out. I could have gone directly to bed, but I really needed to eat something. And there was the name. I didn't think Randy would care how it happened. I didn't want to sound like I was being overly dramatic.

"I came up with a name for the baby."

"Mmm."

"Amber."

"Hmm?"

"It reminds me of Aunt Bernice. Aunt Bernie. Amber."

"What if it's a boy?"

"How about Rock?"

"No."

"Stone."

"No."

I put my feet on the living room table, moved my plate onto my lap and grabbed the jar of peanut butter. I might as well have been eating worms the way Randy looked at me.

I stared back for a second. "Is something wrong?"

"That's all fat. You said you were gonna lose weight. Maybe we need to talk about a divorce."

I stood up and screamed, "You are not going to leave me when I'm seven months pregnant!" I looked at Jade, sat down and stared at the television.

Randy stayed silent.

"Jade's going to a birthday party Sunday, and I want to get some shopping done for our summer trip, so Saturday I'll be taking the truck."

"Jordan's headed up. I tell him to bring the 'vette."

~ ~ ~

The next day, I picked Jade up from school. We followed North Beach Road past the Village Green and turned into the parking lot of Mel's Pharmacy. Across the street, a group of white, cottage-like buildings housed Leapin' Lizards, the local toy store.

We crossed the two-lane road, and as we entered, I said hello to the woman at the register. We veered to the left since the right side was filled with kids' clothing. With a quick glance, I didn't see anything. I figured Bret had enough plastic lizards and trucks, but Jade loved to look at everything so I waited patiently. The shop owner's golden retriever ambled over to greet us, then went back to his post by the register.

We left, undecided, which was fine since we were planning to go to the mainland the next day. We circled back on Prune Alley and Rose Street to stop by the library.

Jade rushed in and headed straight to the shelves of videos. I followed and scanned the titles, hoping she could find a couple of new ones. She collected the allotment of five quickly, then followed me to library catalogue so I could search for a couple of books.

I looked for books with "God" in the title, but noticed some used the word, "spiritual." I thought I understood what it meant, but as I scanned book after book they seemed to be focused more on subjects like healing, love, and zen. I read *Zen and the Art of Motorcycle Maintenance* in high school and didn't get much from it.

I didn't even know what to call what was happening to me, but it wasn't like it was a huge problem. I was dealing with lots of other things closer to home.

I wandered the aisles and found books like: *Family Ties that Bind*, *Bradshaw On: The Family*, *Asimov's Guide to the Bible*, and *What Do You Care What Other People Think?*, so I grabbed them.

Before we left, I scanned the reader board and noticed a monthly writer's group. Saturday mornings. 11:00 a.m. to 1:00 p.m. I thought, *Maybe someday.*

## ~ S E A G U L L S ~

At 8:00 a.m. the next morning, I drove the truck down to the ferry landing and walked home on the water side. The dirt path was only a couple of feet wide so I was always terrified that an earthquake would take me down the 100-foot cliff that was barely keeping the madrones upright, but there wasn't even that much of a path on the other side around a blind curve just before the meadow.

Jade and I walked back about half an hour before the ferry's arrival. The meadow grass was long, yielding slightly to the breeze that rolled over Shaw Island. I tried to appreciate the walk, but twice that morning felt like a lot, so I slowed down as we made our way up the hill to the village. The ferry was pulling out of the landing at Shaw, so I knew we didn't have to hurry, but it was taking more energy than I expected to climb the hill, and there was another one to get up to the parking lot.

Once we boarded, we went up to the passenger deck on the port side, which would have a view of Mt. Baker if it wasn't shrouded in clouds.

Jade picked a spot near the video games, climbed into one of the driver seats, and pretended to steer the cars around the track while I put our belongings in a seat nearby. I scooted in and pulled out *Family Ties That Bind.*

Within a couple of minutes, familiar words were staring me in the face, *I want you to think differently* [1]

I scanned through the book and found language that I'd never put together or applied to my life and my relationships: closeness/distancing, thinking/ feeling, unspoken rules, and differentiating or "this is me, like it or not." [2]

I barely made it through the first chapter when Jade climbed into the seat across from me.

"Can we play *Go Fish?*"

"Sure."

I put the book in my bag and grabbed the card deck. Jade shuffled them, gave us each seven, then put the stack in the middle.

As we approached the Lopez Ferry Terminal, I pointed out Mount Baker. The morning sun was blinding, so we moved to the other side. Shortly after we made our way through the passage between Blakely and Decatur, I could see Mount Rainier. Almost two hundred miles away, the 14,000-foot mass of rock and ice crystals didn't look much bigger than one of Jade's eyeteeth.

A couple of seagulls flew alongside the ferry. One stood on the railing. I loved their calls wherever I was. It made me feel like home was close by.

Jade wanted to feed the birds so we gathered our things and headed to the back of the boat, past the covered, open-air seating, out onto the starboard viewing platform. It was a little too cold for me, so I handed Jade the granola while I stepped back into the covered space.

## ~ M I N D S P A C E . 3 1 ~

I won a small ceramic seagull at a sailing club fundraiser. It still sits in my kitchen. I never felt like I could call what happened with it a miracle, but it did seem like it was out of the ordinary.

When Randy and I arrived at the fundraiser, we had to walk by the prize table where they were selling raffle tickets. I saw the seagull's huge friendly eyes and immediately thought, *I want it.*

Of course I also thought, *That's not going to happen,* as Randy paid for our tickets, then wound his way through the rows of tables looking for a place to sit. I followed closely; thankful I didn't have to make the decision.

Randy could talk "boat" with anyone, so he sat down next to a couple of people that weren't part of the power player set, while I had no idea how to start a conversation with any of them. After a few minutes we went to get food.

As was often the case, fruit was my only option. Thankfully we arrived late, so as I worked my way through my grapes, pineapple, and strawberries, they started to call raffle numbers.

One by one people collected their items as everyone clapped and cheered. When they pulled a ticket for the seagull, I looked at my numbers, and there it was. But then I didn't want to go get it. It was embarrassing. It was such a useless little thing.

When I sat back down, I couldn't help but think, *I asked and I received*, but I also knew that it didn't happen with everything.

## ~ O T | N T ~

Toys-R-Us was in Bellingham. About an hour-long drive. As we drove through Old Town Anacortes, Jade asked me if I could get out her Calico Critters and Woody. I pulled into a gas station parking lot and filled up while we were stopped.

Ask and thou shalt receive.

Jade was and wasn't one of those things. I wanted children, twelve, when I was a child myself. I also wanted to be a professional singer and a naturopath. None of that happened.

I also didn't ask God to introduce me to someone who practically wanted to live on a sailboat. I was usually either terrified, cold, or uncomfortable. But it gave me lots of time to read.

## ~ M I N D S P A C E . 2 9 ~

A couple of years before Jade was born, I realized I didn't have any idea what was in the *Old Testament*, so I decided to read the *Bible* from cover to cover to see if that would help me understand what I seemed to be missing, why I never felt comfortable in church.

I brought the copy my parents gave me as we made our way to the San Juan Islands one summer. When I finished "Ezekiel," Randy asked me what I thought about the wheeled vehicle. We talked about it for a few minutes. He had never expressed his beliefs outright, but it made me happy to know that Randy was familiar with some of it.

After months of grueling effort, I quit about 100 pages short of the *New Testament*. It was such a miserable experience, I decided all I needed to do was skim the *New Testament* since I recognized most of the stories.

One evening when we were at anchor, as Randy and I were enjoying the glowing peach and gray ember-like effect that we often got with Pacific Northwest sunsets, Randy said it meant we were going to have good weather the next day. He chirped, "Red sky at night, sailor's delight. Red sky in the morning, sailors take warning." Then he said, "You know, it's in the *Bible*."

I couldn't remember seeing it in the *Old Testament*. Clearly, I was still missing some things, but the question was, *Did it matter enough to try to hack through content I'd heard about all of my life?*


## ~ V E R T I G O ~


As Jade and I passed through the towering conifers that framed sheared off stone flanking the freeway south of Bellingham, I decided I was finally ready to give the *New Testament* another try. Maybe even read the 100 pages of the *Old Testament* I'd skipped. I'd have lots of time on our next sailing trip.

"We're almost there," I said to Jade.

We pulled into the Toys 'R Us parking lot and got a quick drink before going in. The entrance was filled with an assortment of toys, so we spent a few minutes scanning for ideas, then we walked up and down the aisles.

We finally settled on a Hot Wheels track. Jade had a collection of cars from the grocery store, so she loved the idea. Then we got her a couple of video games and sticker books. When we got back to the car, we had some apples and cheese, then we headed back down the freeway.

Our next stop was Michael's in Mount Vernon. We picked up felt, beads, and rick-rack so we could make holiday ornaments.

Our last stop was the grocery store. We loaded up with canned goods, jerky, fruit juice, and granola bars. Randy told me that there wouldn't be any place to buy food where we were headed this year.

~ ~ ~

Randy was next on the ferry-go-round, getting supplies for his business. I shuffled work with a couple of cleaning projects since a few friends were coming to our place next weekend.

I put the birds out on their perches and started sweeping the deck. Mats of leaves from the shade maple on the southeast side of the house and pine needles from the evergreens on the north had wedged themselves between the planks.

I went around to the street side of the deck, a narrow walkway where we stored the BBQ in the winter. I pushed it away from the house to sweep around it, then decided to move it to the back, since it needed cleaning. It rumbled along, and I thought, *That's really loud.* As soon as I turned the corner with it, Kiroc flew off.

I forget to attach her cable.

I stood there for a minute in disbelief, then I headed into the house and made my way down the spiral staircase and out the door. I only had to take a few steps in the opposite direction to get out of the gate, but all I could think was, *I'm not moving fast enough.*

I looked across the meadow and couldn't see her. I stumbled through the shin-high grass calling her name when I saw an eagle circling. I thought, *I can't do this. I can't watch an eagle take her.*

I kept going, thinking, *What if she reached the water?*

When I got to the swan pond, I scanned the marina, then I ran around the far side of the house. As I went through the yard, looking around the edges of the pond, I was thankful the house was usually empty.

I looked up and saw Kiroc in the trees at least thirty feet above me, which was about fifty feet away from the marina and about seventy-five feet away from the passage that connected to the sea. If she flew off again the wrong way, she could still land in the water.

I didn't know what to do, but thankfully one of our neighbors, who had recently moved into the house in front of the marina saw me running and called out.

"It's Kiroc! I forgot to secure her cable! She's in the tree above the pond. I don't know what to do. Randy's off island!"

"I'll call the Fire Department!"

"Thank you! Could you please tell them there's an eagle circling?"

A few minutes later she was back on her deck. "At first they said they wouldn't come! Then I told them you were alone and seven months pregnant. They should be here in a few minutes!"

I watched Kiroc, praying that they would be able to get her. Praying that she wouldn't fly off in the wrong direction.

I called for her, but knew she wouldn't listen. She tolerated me, but loved Randy.

When the firemen arrived, they raised a huge ladder. The fireman tried to talk to her, but she wouldn't budge. After about ten minutes, he started shaking the branch. I thought, *What are her chances of making it out of there safely?*

The fireman gave it another good shake and off she went, heading toward the bay. I ran back around the far side of the house and found her in the middle of the street, apparently too tired from her first adventure to make it any farther. I thanked the firemen and my neighbor, then I walked back up the road holding tightly onto Kiroc's leathery toes. I had a few minutes to collect myself before I had to leave to pick up Jade. After I put both birds in their cages, I curled up on the couch.

## ~ M I N D S P A C E . 2 7 ~

I had no idea what it meant to own a macaw before we got Kiroc. I had parakeets when Randy and I met, and I assumed having a macaw would be the same. We could leave for weekends and vacation without worry.

Looking at a bird, it seems like it would be impossible to tell how they're feeling, but when we got back from vacation one year, I could. Kiroc's body was slumped, her eyes vacant.

I talked to Randy about getting her a companion. I wanted another Blue & Gold, but he wanted something different. We found a breeder in North Seattle, and one of the Green Wings snuggled up to me like I was its best friend.

Kiroc barely tolerated Rocket for over a year. Then one day when they were outside climbing around a cast iron table, Kiroc backed up to Rocket. We had a male and a female.

When Kiroc and Rocket began to communicate with each other and with me, about each other, I got a better understanding of how intelligent they were, but I couldn't change anything at that point.

## ~ A N  A L T E R N A T E  U N I V E R S E ~

It looked like we were going to have a perfect evening. The sky surrounding the billowing clouds was so blue it looked like you could dive right in.

Randy and Steve were outside cleaning crab when Kevin and Kimberly arrived. A small chapel to the north of Kevin's place hosted a lot of wedding parties, so he was building guest cottages, and Randy spent lots of time helping him. They didn't have children, and there never seemed to be an opportunity to talk to Kimberly alone. Kevin was a self-assured, walking trombone. He didn't preach, but his speech flickered with fire and brimstone, so I kept my distance.

Jordan and Jessica had arrived the night before so they'd gone to Eastsound to check out the shops and buy some provisions for their stay on our boat. Shortly after Randy and Steve came in with the five-gallon cooking pot brimming with crab, Jordan pulled into the driveway.

Tina followed Randy and Steve. I offered them a glass of wine. It was either Pinot Noir from the Oregon Coast or Chardonnay. I didn't drink Chardonnay. I just read labels and took my chances. I poured Pinot for Randy and Chardonnay for Steve and Tina. Then I poured myself half an inch of Pinot in a cordial glass and usually had half of that left by the end of the evening.

Tina was distant at times, but at others willing to connect. She didn't have children, but she always spent time with Jade, which I appreciated. The conversation continued to revolve around the crab until Jordan and Jess came in.

Jordan bellowed, "Let's get this party started!" and dropped a case of Corona on the teak dining room table. Almost every time I saw Jordan, he had a different girlfriend. But once in a while one of the previous ones showed up. I'd met Jess before. She was one of the most beautiful women I had ever seen. Huge blue eyes and long black hair that fell around her face in waves. I wondered if this meant she might be sticking around for a while.

Denny and Zola were the first people Randy met on the island. They owned the souvenir shop in the village and a resort in Eastsound. I could see them coming down the ramp as I put the birds in their cages.

Denny set a bottle of Jack Daniels on the table next to the Corona, took a glass of Pinot Noir I held out for him, and wandered out to the back deck where the guys had migrated. "Hi, my lovelies," Zola said, walking over to give Jade a hug. She seemed to be at home almost anywhere.

"Hi, Zola! Glad you could make it."

Zola was an unusual woman. A force unlike anything I'd ever seen. She was tiny, but had an incredible amount of energy and a heart big enough for everyone.

I wasn't quite sure what to make of her when we first moved to the island. She talked about so many different people it was hard to keep up. Island politics. Who's who in the neighborhood. Family issues. I didn't feel like I could connect with her very well, but it was difficult not to be pulled into her circle. She was Christian, but surprisingly open-minded. She understood the needs of the women, young and old, in the community, and she accepted other people's beliefs. To a point. One of her sisters had married a man from the Mormon faith, and she was constantly frustrated by the situation.

## ~MINDSPACE.11~

I had a friend from fifth grade who belonged to the Mormon faith, so I felt like I could understand, at least a little. The first time I went to Naomi's house, she told me she didn't drink Coca-Cola® and only ate one square of a bar of chocolate. It was like stepping into an alternate universe. She talked me into trying Pluto Water, which quenched any further curiosity on my part. Not long afterward, Naomi and I had a disagreement that ended our friendship.

Years later, when I was home from college during Christmas break, Naomi showed up at my parents' doorstep. We talked for hours and began to send letters. At one point she included a copy of the *Mormon Bible*, but for years, I was afraid to open it.

~ ~ ~

Jade was enjoying Zola's attention while I shuffled around the kitchen, warming focaccia in the oven and putting a charcuterie board on the table. I put tongs Randy made for Christmas gifts a few years before across the lip of a large salad bowl and took it out to the table. Then I grabbed the case of Corona and put it in the fridge.

The crab pot had come to a boil, so I set a timer for five minutes and let Randy know. Zola was reading to Jade so I sat down on the couch and curled my feet up to relax for a few minutes.

## ~MINDSPACE.37~

I decided to "read" the *Mormon Bible* around the time I finally walked away from Christianity. I was back in search mode. If someone asked me how I felt about books, I probably would have said they were sacred. Words that found their way into books had a tremendous impact on people, so I was stunned, or perhaps more saddened, as I tried to process the "First Book of Nephi."

It was like reading something written by a 12-year-old. I wondered how anyone could take it seriously. Then I found out Joseph Smith was actually 14.

What first stood out to me was Nephi's use of the word, things, a word I used a lot when I started writing. But it's like giving people counterfeit money. Sure, they get something, but they can't do anything with it.

## ~BRASH~

The crab was cool enough to crack. Everyone lined up to grab a half, along with bread, accouterments, and salad, and found a place to sit either at the dining room table or outside. I sat at the far end of the dining room table and cracked crab for Jade, then started on half a crab for me. Jade crawled into the seat beside me, and I put a large segment of one of the claws in her mouth, getting a big grin. Then I went and dropped a couple of segments into the bird dishes so they could join in.

Jade offered me something a never imagined I would get from a child. A kind of a force field that allowed me to separate myself from the crowd.

I was always attentive to her needs, but in the spaces between, I found that I was often able to withdraw enough from the lure of the group conversations —no longer believing I would miss something or think I was required to be there—to observe and follow my own thoughts. Since I wasn't a drinker, an avid sailor, a mechanic, or a socialite, no one expected much from me. I was able to listen or tune out with relative ease.

As time went on, I began to openly excuse myself from some of the conversations. I started calling them "amps." "If you guys are going to talk about amps again…." Of course, amps are important on a boat. Battery amps. Marine-grade amplifiers. The electrical system provides the life blood to their passion. But there was another reason I stopped being able to tolerate many of the stories. Denny brought a reminder.

We'd been out on the sailboat with a couple of friends and the guys drank an entire bottle of Jack Daniels. A short time later when they were together again, Randy said, "We downed an entire bottle." The guy said, "Each!" Everyone laughed but me. I was there. I knew what happened, while Randy shot me that look: Don't. Say. A. Word.

I got up and put on Edgar Winter, *They Only Come Out at Night.*

~ ~ ~

I wondered why it mattered. Why some people felt the need to amp up their stories. It was everywhere in Joseph Smith's writing.

Nephi uses the word, "things," twelve times in the first chapter (I started counting after three). The thing is, the word, things, didn't exist at the time.

Lehi, Nephi's father, says he does things "on behalf of his people." But the only people around were his immediate family.[3]

Nephi kills a man to get the plates of brass or gold (Mormons aren't sure which).

Alma, a "prophet who lived around the year of approx. 150 years BC," said they only followed the law of Moses, "Thou shalt not kill," because it was "expedient." They describe the law of Moses in a similar way to (Christ's) coming, so they kept up those "outward performances" until that time.[4]

In my early work as a graphic designer, I often counted words per page to estimate project lengths. The *Mormon Bible,* weighing in at roughly 267,000 words, would fill about 900 pages in 12-point Times. That would require a lot of gold or brass (which was only available in large quantities starting around 1850 AD), even if it had been rendered in some ancient form of shorthand hieroglyphics.

Maybe there haven't ever been any sailors that follow the Mormon faith, but for some strange reason I'd become one, and I realized as Nephi talked about sailing to the promised land, that the Red Sea is about 10,000 nautical miles from Florida. The farthest I'd traveled on a boat in one direction was about 200. At six knots, propelled by a motor, it took three to four days depending on the tides. At that speed, it would have taken Nephi's family at least half a year. Without any canned food.

The keel on our boat was 5,000 lbs. What did Nephi use? How did they move the boat from the land to the water?

Nephi said they found horses in America. But historical records say they became extinct about 10,000 years ago and were reintroduced in the U.S. in 1519 by Columbus.[5]

~ ~ ~

It's easy to put our minds on autopilot and miss all of this. Or avoid questions to appease someone else. I found myself doing it, too. It wasn't like there was a line winched around my neck keeping me from speaking freely. I wondered, *How are so many of us held in line like this?*

~ ~ ~

*Frankenstein* started to play so I turned up the volume. Jade swayed to and fro, but it wasn't dance music. It was more like an experience. Rock n' roll meets Star Trek.

Everyone had come inside. Sitting on the couch and leather chairs around the fireplace. Randy prepared after-dinner drinks. Shots for those that wanted them. Jade was apparently bored, needing some attention. She started twirling in the space between the glass table and the fireplace. Everyone was commenting about how cute she was.

As a kid, I twirled. I knew what happened when you twirled. But I just sat there, watching. I don't know if I was trying to enjoy her enjoying the moment or if I was just too tired to realize what was coming.

Then I was in that agonizing moment when I saw her start to fall, when I knew I couldn't span the distance fast enough. I reached her just as her forehead hit and stopped her from falling farther. I swooped her up and ran to the bedroom. A few minutes later someone came in and told me to watch her eyes, to make sure she didn't have a concussion.

I was furious with myself. I wanted to go throw my head against the table. I cuddled up to Jade on the bed and apologized over and over.

There was still a hint of blue in the sky. A deep, midnight blue that always drew me in. As I stared out the sliding glass doors, I could hear bits and pieces of the conversation in the living room. They were talking about the trip. Steve and Tina had already been there. Tina said that they took her parents with them one year and didn't know they needed to wait for slack tide before going through the southern passage, Surge Narrows. She said she thought they were going to die.

I'd been in some uncomfortable situations, so I had a good idea of what it was like. I wanted to walk out and say, "Why don't we go somewhere else?" but I figured the guys wanted to go just for the thrill.

About an hour later Jade seemed to be okay. We got up and went out to the couch. After everyone left, Randy told me everyone had settled on a date. The third weekend in August.

As we were getting ready for bed, Randy said he would get something that would work as a guard around the table's edge on his next trip off island.

~ L I O N ~

As the days passed by in June and early July, I was hoping the baby would be born under a water sign. I still didn't "believe in astrology" so I couldn't understand why it mattered. The last possible day passed. Still, it gnawed at me.

A couple of days later at about 11:00 p.m., I pushed myself back into the curve of the couch and did something I'd never done. I asked Randy to hand me my glass of water. What was stranger still, a few minutes later, I asked him to hand me a plate from the table, and he was farther away from it than I was. He asked me if anything was wrong, and I said, "No, I'm just tired."

I sat there in an unusual state of satisfaction and noticed my body had stopped hurting. Finally, I could relax. A few minutes later the ache came back. As spans of only minutes passed between the ebb and flow of pain, the message from my body was clear. I complained, "I don't want to go through this at night."

I'd heard that the second child would be faster, easier. Within a couple of hours, I was being driven to my knees. The midwife and I flew off into the darkness to the hospital in Anacortes.

The pain continued to increase, and the contractions were close together. Instead of the marathon I had gone through with Jade, this felt more like a sprint. There was so little time to catch my breath when another contraction would start to build. I protested with everything in me. Not with lovely feminine screams. I roared. I didn't care if the entire world knew what was happening. It felt right to let my body express that energy in all of its intensity.

At about four in the morning, the midwife left my side, leaving me clutching the inanimate railing. Minutes later, Randy and Jade walked in. Randy stepped up to the side of the bed, and I grabbed his arm, bearing down into the elasticity of his flesh.

Jade heard my screams, and I wondered what she was thinking. I was beyond exhaustion, telling the nurses I couldn't do anything. Then, suddenly, my diaphragm created a tremendous thrust.

The next thing I saw was Jade sitting in a chair holding her baby sister. I felt a mix of happiness and terror as she sat there, the first one of us to hold Amber. She looked at me with an ever-so-slightly furrowed brow, making me think she felt the same way, then the nurse took Amber and brought her to me.

I'm not sure when I finally found out she'd been born under the sign of the lion. I was disappointed. But I could only think of one reason--it wasn't very feminine.

As if a crab was.

~ ~ ~

But a crab has to molt, and when that happens, they're soft, vulnerable. I seemed to go through periods where I had to endure painful transitions, then I lived for long periods of time in states where I became hardened, even combative.

At some points I felt more like a man than a woman. When I had to walk home alone, I tucked my hair in my coat and tried to walk like a man. When I looked in the mirror one day, the face that looked back was male. I spent years struggling with a couple of dreams where I was in a grade school restroom trying to figure out what to do with a penis between my legs.

I did a lot of stupid things to try to prove I was as tough as the guys. Sneaking out at night. Opening beer bottles with my teeth. Racing. I did, and I didn't care what people thought of me, but I didn't believe I could change.

## ~ T O R T U R E ~

Two weeks after Amber arrived, we headed to the Octopus Islands.

Randy could single-hand the boat like it was an extension of him, but that didn't mean it was easy for long-hauls. After we moved and began to sail farther north, which meant being exposed to the Georgia Straits, we started to make other arrangements. We would find someone to accompany him, then I drove up to meet him in Lund, the last stop on Highway 101.

Royce, Marcie, and Jordan offered to help with this trip. Royce would take the boat north with Randy, and Marcie would drive me and the girls to Lund, then they would drive home together. I would leave our truck at the Anacortes Ferry Terminal, and Jordan would leave his car there, as well. He would drive our truck to Lund, so I could take the kids home in it, then he would help Randy bring the boat home. The drive included three ferry rides so I figured I could make it back alone.

Randy picked up Royce on one of his supply runs and figured they could make the trip in three days. Steve and Tina headed up to Nanaimo a few days earlier in their 30-foot Pearson so they could cross the straits together.

At 8:00 a.m., the next Saturday morning, Marcie and I met at the Anacortes Ferry Terminal. I had run until nearly 1:00 a.m. trying to get everything ready, then I had to get the three of us up to catch the 6:45 a.m. sailing. I pulled into the parking lot, then we transferred our belongings to Marcie's trunk. We'd crossed the Swinomish Channel, and I was just beginning to relax when I realized I hadn't paid for parking. We had to turn back.

Thankfully, when we reached Horseshoe Bay, just to the north of Vancouver, we were able to practically drive right onto the ferry. That gave Jade about an hour to run around and explore, and me time to take care of Amber. The route continued up the Sunshine Coast with the landscape becoming more and more mountainous as we followed the coastline and passed through small, scattered towns.

Earls Cove, the location of the next terminal, was a dot in the wilderness. A handful of buildings that included a restaurant and gift shop. I fed Amber, then we got out for a stretch. Jade found a stuffed deer that she desperately wanted, while I stood there thinking, *No more stuffed animals*, but Marcie offered to buy it for her.

When we reached Saltery Bay, we were only about an hour away from Lund, but as we followed the narrow, curvy road, it felt like it was taking longer. We finally began to see a few homes alongside the road, so I knew we were getting close, then we passed Nancy's Bakery, and the clearing came into view.

After we loaded everything onto the boat, I stayed on board with Amber while the rest of the crew went to The Boardwalk Restaurant. It was finally quiet, except for the intermittent waves slapping against the hull.

After Amber fell asleep, I got up and fixed myself a plate of sliced meat, cheese, and cucumber. I went up to the cockpit while I ate and checked out the boats in the harbor. Some had peeling paint. Another had towels hanging over the lifelines. There were a couple of trawlers, but I couldn't tell if they were Grand Banks. Muffled conversations from the restaurant floated over the water and reflections of the outdoor lights looked like a submerged fence.

When the crew got back, I got Jade ready for bed, washed my face, and climbed in, thinking about the big adventure that lay ahead.

~ ~ ~

Royce and Randy didn't waste any time getting underway the next morning, but there wasn't any reason for me to hurry, I'd seen most of it already. We were headed for a small bay at the north end of West Redonda Island to position ourselves for slack tide through Hole in the Wall, the four-mile-long northern entrance to the Octopus Islands.

I waited until everyone else had gotten up, then I curled my hair and put on my makeup.

As we made our way north, Jade ran up and down the steps from the cabin to the cockpit. She'd spend a little time on deck, then join me to work on a project. Even though it was painful to feel like I had to wait until Jade was independent to talk to Randy about having a second child, I was so thankful she was doing so well with it.

When we reached Redonda Bay, the guys set anchor. They got out fishing poles, and I prepared lunch. Steve and Tina anchored close enough that everyone could comfortably talk.

Royce came down to grab the Tide Tables.

After a few minutes I heard him say, "Are they on daylight savings?"

"Should be," Randy replied.

"Then we need to go through at 3:20."

Steve called out, "We don't have the same power you've got under your hood. I hope you're right."

"I'm sure," Randy replied.

We planned to meet at the entrance so we could make sure it was slack, so I felt like we were doing everything we could.

~ ~ ~

After lunch, I crawled into the aft cabin with Amber. I fed her, then got out a couple of toys and attached them to the car seat.

I fished out my copy of the *Bible* and scanned "Maccabees" to see where I left off.

- King Seleucus and the governor, Apollonius, try to seize the gold and silver in a temple in Jerusalem.
- God protected the temple, stopping the governor and his armed forces with angels on horseback and lightening.[6]
- When that king died, his son, Antiochus, overtook the temple and forced the Jewish community to call it the temple of Zeus.[7] Then he tried to eliminate Judaism by forcing every Hebrew to violate their beliefs or endure unimaginable torture.
- As an example of how reason is sovereign over the emotions, the author shares a story of an elderly man and his seven sons who are violently tortured but are able to "retain the virtue of reason" over emotion (torture). The prize: pure and immortal souls in endless life.[8]
- The actions and claims of the wife and mother of these men remind the reader that women are inferior, but tolerated if they are uneducated virgins. She says, "I was a pure virgin and did not go outside my father's house, but I guarded the rib from which woman was made…No seducer corrupted me on a desert plain, nor did the destroyer, the deceitful serpent, defile the purity of my virginity. In the time of my maturity, I remained with my husband…(who) taught (my sons) the law and the prophets."[9]

~ ~ ~

It was incredibly difficult to read. I imagine the purpose was to show the Jewish people they could endure anything to be accepted into Heaven, but then I realized that the angels on horseback only appeared when the Jewish people were trying to stop the King from taking the money. I wondered, *Why didn't angels appear and use lightening to save the old man and his family?*

Because it wasn't real.

It was an amp'ed up story about men being able to speak volumes about the importance of their beliefs even as they endure horrific torture. Of course, torturing one man wasn't enough. They had to add seven "near perfect" sons being able to speak in unison, "as if with one mind".[10] Without this grisly story, they wouldn't be able to praise men for their courage in maintaining their faith, or more importantly the specific beliefs which helped to define their faith, and women for their dedication to maintaining their virtue and seeing their families suffer like this because their religious beliefs were more important.

~ ~ ~

I turned the page and the "prince of peace," Jesus, entered, stage left.

~ ~ ~

"Hot damn! It's a blue!"

"You don't come across those every day."

Jade ran up to see it. Another rockfish. I didn't know why they bothered. To me, they had all the appeal of egg whites.

When it was time for dinner, they put it on foil on the BBQ, then added a couple pork tenderloins while I prepared a corn salad and buttered a loaf of cheese bread. When dinner was finished, everyone (but me) roasted marshmallows.

We left at 1:30 p.m. the next day and circled near Hole in the Wall's entrance looking for signs of visible current. Slack didn't last long. Randy steered in first to see if we were being pulled one way or the other. Seeing that we kept going, Steve and Tina followed. I stayed on the bow and from time to time, the tide gently pulled on the boat. Then, as we neared the narrows on the west side, we started to see whirlpools and eddies. The pull became substantial.

"We're an hour off," Royce said.

"Yeah," I said turning around to see how Steve and Tina were doing. "I'll be calling the coast guard before we go through Surge."

The Octopus Islands were across Okisollo Channel. We anchored in the north bay, and I wondered why everyone made such as fuss. I couldn't see anything special about it, but I was glad to be able to settle in and relax.

The next day Randy and Royce took Jade fishing in the dinghy. Steve and Tina went gunkholing around Waiatt Bay leaving Marcie, Amber, and I. Not long afterward it started to rain. Then it was pouring.

Half an hour went by. The rain continued.

After about an hour it slowed to a drizzle, and I thought, *They should be home. They have to be soaked. This isn't normal.* I started to panic.

I called out to Marcie, "We need to go find them. They should be back."

She tried to calm me down as I paced the deck of the boat, looking out in the distance for signs of them. Another half hour, and I was frantic. Ready to pull anchor, but I knew Marcie and I couldn't do it.

The rain stopped, and they still didn't show up. A couple went by in their dinghy, and I told them I was afraid something bad had happened. They said they would see what they could find.

A short time later, Steve and Tina returned, and they said they hadn't seen them. A few minutes later, the trio appeared.

As they approached, I went below. Marcie told them that I was upset. Jade came down to change her clothes, and I tried to not make a big deal out of it.

It wasn't like Randy did it on purpose.

## ~ M I N D S P A C E . 1 0 ~

Being married to Randy meant sailing was going to be a significant part my life. I figured if we were doing anything else, there would be similar problems. But for most of my life, I had carried around a strange connection to it.

As Randy and I began to spend time together, first on his 20-foot sailboat, then on the others, I couldn't help but think about a song I'd loved since I was a child.

My father's only brother was an English professor. At 10-years old, I noticed something different about him, but I didn't understand exactly what until he visited one day and brought a couple of record albums. I put on "Hair," from The American Tribal Love-Rock Musical, and I loved the energy, but a few days later, I couldn't find it.

The cover of "The Songs of Leonard Cohen," wasn't nearly as intriguing, but I put it on anyway. When I heard "Suzanne," I was overwhelmed. A few years later, when I heard it again, it felt like it had been written about me. I knew it couldn't be, but so much of it rang true.

For years, I puzzled over it. I wanted to connect to every word, but I couldn't. I lived in the desert.

Then I met Randy.

The song continued to surface every once in a while, and while the connection seemed to have deepened, there was a phrase I didn't think I would ever be able to resolve, the line that said, "He (Jesus) sank beneath your wisdom like a stone."

All I could do was keep reminding myself that my feelings were just the musings of a weird child.

## ~ G O  O N ~

I finally started the *New Testament*, but I had to read the third sentence twice.

"…David was the father of Solomon by the wife of Uriah…."[11]

King David's son, Solomon, was conceived through adultery. Really? There weren't any secret words to hide the fact? This was "the" King David that was part of Jesus' genealogy. I read on:

- The iterations of "the father of," stopped when it reached Joseph. He was "the husband of Mary, of whom Jesus was born."[12]

Jesus's lineage from King David and Abraham, the patriarch of the Abrahamic religions, didn't exist. I thought that was enough, then I saw this:

- When the wise men set out to find Jesus, "…there, ahead of them, went the star…until it stopped over the place the child was."[13]

A star stopped.

I thought, *Why would anyone need to read any more?* But on I went.

- The wise men went into a "house," not a manger, and after they left, another angel appeared and told them to go to Egypt.[14]

No manger? I skipped ahead to "Mark" to see if it was there. "Mark" starts with an adult John the Baptizer and an adult Jesus who is famous.[15]

"Luke" apparently thinks he needs to include a little more history so he introduces us to John's the Baptizer's parents, Zechariah and Elizabeth.

Zechariah and Elizabeth are an elderly couple. An angel tells Zechariah that Elizabeth will be bearing a child. Mary and Elizabeth know one another. "Luke" tells us that John leaps in Elizabeth's womb at the sound of Mary's voice. Then when Elizabeth says, "Blessed is the fruit of your womb,"[16] Mary says something I'd never heard:

- "...Surely from now on all generations will call me blessed." This will help "Israel...according to a promise God made to their ancestors and...their descendants forever."[17]

I thought, *No, it didn't. Jesus didn't bring peace to the Jewish people. He created a monumental chasm.*

There was a manger in "Luke," but there weren't any wise men, only shepherds. And they didn't go to Egypt. I skipped ahead to "John."

- "John" starts by introducing God as an abstract concept: "the word."[18] A short time later, he says that "No one has ever seen God."[19]

I thought, *I could have sworn I read that at least a couple of people had seen God.* It didn't take long to find them.

- In "Genesis," God talks directly to Adam and Eve.[20] Adam and Eve have two sons, Cain and Abel. Cain gets angry when God likes Abel's offering and dismisses his, so he kills Abel. As God tells Cain he is being banished, Cain says to God, "I will be hidden from your face." He heads to the land of Nod, and finds a wife.[21]

No one else is supposed to be on the planet. It was hard to think about reading any more, but I figured if I found this much, I should keep going.

~ ~ ~

Amber was asleep and my legs ached. I got up and climbed up and down the companionway stairs a few times. I didn't want to sit anymore, but it was too cold to swim. The guys were trying to catch prawns, and Marcie was sitting in the cockpit reading a magazine.

I could hear Tina on the foredeck. She was relaxing in Randy's hammock, strung up between the forestay and mast. As I crawled around the dodger, I could hear her talking to Jade. I went to the bow and hung my feet over the side under the safety netting. When she finished, she rolled over and said, "We should trade places."

"I need some exercise."

"You could try climbing in and out of this a few times." We both laughed.

"I went up and down the steps a few times before coming up."

"I just remembered I meant to bring you a book. About motherhood. It's a collection of poems. I'll get it to you when we get back."

"That sounds great."

I was conflicted about poetry. It was an expression of a moment, and I had way too much going on in my head. Tina didn't have children. Maybe she felt like the book needed a better home.

"Did you bring your ukulele?"

"No, people have to put with enough of that at parties."

"I've always wanted to play the Mandolin."

"Then you should get one."

"Funds are a little tight."

She lowered her voice and cupped her hand, "That doesn't stop Randy. It shouldn't stop you from doing something nice for yourself."

~ ~ ~

I didn't leave the boat during our stay. I rested, read, and helped with food preparation. As we made plans to leave the area, the storage bins were still crammed full. A couple of times, I heard Randy talking about how much shopping I had done. I spent hours creating menus so we wouldn't run out, and we hadn't gone any farther than the north side of an island that had one of Desolation's main grocery stores.

As we were pulling anchor, I hailed the coastguard. The Tide Tables were not on daylight savings time.

I asked them twice to tell me when slack tide was in Surge Narrows. I imagine they were annoyed, but I didn't care.

As we approached the passage, a couple of boats were waiting. We held back until they proceeded, then we followed through a passage hardly wide enough for two boats to pass in the opposite direction. The water was still creating whirlpools around the exposed rocks.

We motored around Read Island and headed to Von Donop Inlet on the west side of Cortes. Randy said there was a fairly level trail from there to Squirrel Cove, one of my favorite places.

We anchored near towering trees so there wasn't anything to see. Jade and I went below and closed the cabin doors to keep out the mosquitos.

We had prawns and oysters in a natural cooler—a net hanging off the aft end, so Randy lit the BBQ. I boiled red potatoes, made a quick cabbage salad, then I put out olives, dill cream cheese, smoked salmon, and mini-bagels for hors d'oeuvres while Tina held Amber. After dinner, Jade and I worked on a felting project and read books together as the rest of the crew uncorked a bottle of wine and figured out whose turn it was to wash dishes. I went back to the aft cabin to feed Amber, then I finished reading Matthew, underlining phrases I remembered and a few things that stood out, like the fact that:

- Matthew mentioned multiple times that Jesus casts out demons.

No one, in any church I'd ever attended, mentioned demons. Real demons. That people could see.

- After his death, Jesus "appears to the disciples" and says, "All authority in heaven and on earth has been given to me."[22]

Suddenly one plus one didn't equal one. If Jesus and God were one from the beginning, why would Jesus say that?

~ ~ ~

Marcie made breakfast before our hike to Squirrel Cove. Eggs with bacon and cheese. Everyone lollygagged over coffee while I took care of cleanup, then the guys set out prawn traps. Royce started talking about food again, so we decided to get going. Randy ferried Royce and Marcie to shore. Then Jade, Amber, and me. Steve and Tina decided to stay on their boat, so Royce hauled the dingy up into the trailhead, which made disembarking easy.

Randy and Royce took turns giving Jade piggy-back rides when she got tired, and I carried Amber in a sling. The path ended near a restaurant, so we went inside to get lunch. Jade ordered a hotdog, but she was willing to try some of my calamari. After we finished, we hiked around the rocky cove to the general store to browse for a while. Jade found a book she liked, and she got ice cream before we headed back.

We decided to prepare an easy dinner. Apples, cheese, salami, and crackers. The guys settled in with their drinks, and I called it a day.

~ ~ ~

Steve and Randy got underway again at about 7:00 am. The trip around the north end of West Redonda and down Waddington Channel was uninspiring, but Pendrell Sound was one of the most beautiful places in the area. Its most outstanding feature was clear water that averaged about 20- to 25-degrees warmer than any other place in the Pacific Northwest.

Randy set the anchor, then Royce rowed to shore to attach a stern line that allowed Steve and Tina to anchor close by. While Amber was sleeping, Jade and I put on swimsuits and lifejackets and bobbed in and out of the water on the swim step. Tina swam over to meet us, while the rest of the crew went to gather more oysters. We enjoyed a lazy afternoon, then we backtracked up Waddington Channel to Walsh Cove for the evening in preparation for our next venture: Toba Inlet.

~ ~ ~

Homfray Channel, the southerly route home once you passed the north end of East Rodonda Island, was one of the most breathtaking stretches I'd ever seen. Mountains literally rose from the sea. Toba Inlet was north, northeast of that passage.

The hillsides were a concurrence of waterfalls. The sea beneath, soft green, glacial. It was so deep near the shoreline, we could put the bow of the boat directly into some of them.

We chased waterfalls into the early afternoon, but when Amber and I had gotten enough sun, I took her below. A short time later the crew turned around and headed to the Malaspina Provincial Park at the south end of Homfray. It was the last stop before the short jaunt back to Lund.

The next day, I spent most of the time below with Amber. Randy, Royce, and Steve took Jade out for a dinghy ride early in the day. Marcie and Tina took turns holding Amber while I cleaned and sorted our belongings. When the dinghy crew returned, they were full of excitement. They had seen a black bear. Bears were the main reason we didn't hike in the area.

Tina went on an almost daily swim. When she got back, she spent some time with Jade in the hammock again. Everyone else was in the cockpit with afternoon cocktails or beer, so I worked my way through "Mark."

~ ~ ~

Demons were now speaking directly to Jesus, telling him that they "knew he was the Holy One, the Son of God." [23] I took breaks in between some of the sections to stretch or rest. After a while, I noticed that I was reading the same stories I had seen in "Matthew."

- The heavens open up when Jesus was baptized.
- The Kingdom had come near.
- Jesus spoke with authority.
- Withered hand.
- Sower parable.
- Divorce.
- Calming the sea.
- The eye of the needle.
- When the cock crowed.
- "Are you the King of the Jews?"
- A passer-by carried Jesus's cross.
- Sponge with sour wine.
- "My God, my God, why have you forsaken me?"
- The temple curtain tears in two.

Word for word. As though they had been copied and pasted.

As if "Mark" noticed that "Matthew" left out John the Baptist's story, so he started with that, then he copied and pasted the middle, changing the sequence in a few places so it was hard to tell. Then he added an ending with more punch:

- People who believed that Jesus was the savior could safely drink poison.[24]

I moved forward to "Luke."

~ ~ ~

"Luke" included the same stories. The slow drip was wearing on me. But when I reached Luke 4.25, I felt like I'd stumbled upon a secret cache that people throughout the ages had been too arrogant to realize needed to be buried.

- Jesus was in a synagogue telling people that not everyone gets healed. He said, "Heaven was shut up three years and six months" during the time of Elijah.[25]

My brain felt like it was going to explode. I was too tired to keep reading. I was disappointed. I was hoping I'd be finished. I took Amber up to the cockpit, and Tina offered to hold her while I did more cleaning.

A sailboat is like an inverted vacuum cleaner. Debris is constantly sucked in through an open forward hatch or open companionway doors, then dropped. I shook out the runner carpets, swept, and dusted. Then Marcie helped me fix dinner. Afterwards, I gathered up all of the things Jade and I had out for our projects. We'd be back on the road tomorrow.

~ ~ ~

Everyone was up at 6:00 a.m. The only clouds in the area were nestled close to the horizon. We made it to Lund in a little over two hours and tied up at one of the docks. Jordan stayed overnight in Powell River and arrived about 30 minutes later. Royce and Marcie drove off as soon as they were sure Jordan was going to make it. I didn't think I'd be able to keep up with them with the kids anyway.

As Jordan settled in, Jade and I went to the store to get some fresh food for the trip home.

Souvenirs and candy crowded the entry. Jade hesitated so she could get a quick look, then followed me. I grabbed local blueberries and a couple of apples, then we went over to the deli counter to order sliced meat and cheese. While the clerk was packaging the food, I looked over the candy selection.

"Do you want a rainbow lollipop?"

Jade smiled and grabbed one that she could reach. It wasn't the biggest, but it was big enough for her. I looked around and saw a container of playing cards.

"Let's get some new cards. Pick whatever you want."

Jade rummaged through them, pushing aside ones with illustrations by Coast Salish Kwakiutl First Nations, some with Canadian maple leaves, and others that were designed as trail guides, and found a standard red deck. I liked the First Nations designs, but kept my opinion to myself.

I put the food in a cooler in the back of the truck, then we went back to the boat so I could feed Amber. Jade stayed on deck and told Jordan about the hikes, waterfalls, and bear. After we said goodbye to Tina, Steve, and Jordan, Randy carried Amber and her car seat up to the truck.

~ ~ ~

We wound our way back along the two-lane highway that ran low along the coastline. Thankfully we were able to catch ferries within reasonable wait times, then we pulled into the Langdale Ferry Terminal. Seventeen lanes across and a quarter of a mile long. A radical contrast to transition us back to civilization. I couldn't help but feel an immense sense of emptiness.

After we passed through customs, the scenery became familiar, and I felt the pull of home. I wanted to be there that moment, to be able to see Kiroc and Rocket. I was the person that made their lives bearable. I hated being away any longer than I had to.

## ~ P A T H W A Y S ~

About a month later, at five and a half, Jade started Kindergarten. I'd been told by one of Randy's friends that no one would let a child start at four, so I hadn't tried.

One morning, when Amber and I got home after taking Jade to school, I took her to the changing station before we headed down to my office. The light must have been coming through the bathroom window just right because I hadn't noticed that she actually had gray eyes with a broad, yellow band that flared out around the pupil, often making them look green.

"Where did you come from, child of mine?" I said to her. "I see the sun shine in your eyes. A whirling mass of time we share. Days melt into night."

The poem kept going. When it seemed to be finished, it felt like a bookmark, a life placeholder. Something that would help me remember the moment.

I wondered about the process of writing sometimes. Words just appeared like something had cracked open inside. Not something that would leave a scar, something that etched a permanent, beautiful pathway.

I shared the poem with a few members of my family and friends, but I wasn't sure about the last line, "Dawn of promise, guide you well. Grow strong as we grow apart," when one of them said, "But you'll always have a connection with your children."

## ~ S C H O O L E D ~

I was sitting in the truck in the Elementary School parking lot trying to force myself to stop thinking about all of the issues that were happening with family. I couldn't seem to talk on the phone or join family gatherings without something awful happening. One of the worst was over the Christmas holiday. When we visited Randy's mother, she called him by his first and middle name. When he called out from the kitchen to remind her that he had changed his middle name to my maiden name, I was to blame. She came after me, and I wasn't able to sleep. There wasn't anything I could do to fix that kind of thing, so I carried them with me. Every issue, no matter how small, made me feel terrible.

Amber was finally starting to sleep better, so I was trying to be thankful that at least one stress was ebbing. As I tried to shift my focus, I noticed the progress the students had made on their vegetable garden at the west edge of the school property.

Then I noticed a woman rushing toward me. Her faded red hair flowing behind her almost horizontally. I figured she was going to pass by, but she stopped at the window.

I rolled it down.

"Are you Jade's mother?"

My heart started pounding. I nodded, afraid of what she was going to say.

"It's nothing urgent," she said apparently seeing me grimace and brace for the impact. "I'm the assistant teacher in Jade's class. I've been wanting to talk to you for a long time. I wanted to let you know she doesn't belong there."

"Oh. O-okay," I sputtered, trying to regain my composure. "Thanks."

"Of course. It's just that she's really far ahead of the other kids."

"I heard that schools wouldn't let anyone start Kindergarten at four, so I didn't talk to anyone. But thank you. I appreciate it."

"You're welcome. I'm sorry I didn't say something sooner," she said as she spun around.

"No worries. Thanks, again," I called out as she disappeared into the crowd of kids flowing out the doors.

I thought, *It's late spring. We can't do anything. We couldn't have done anything anyway. Randy's friend said the cutoff was sometime in November.*

Jade came bounding across the grass, so I went around to the other side of the truck and opened the crew cab door.

"How did school go today?"

"Good."

"Amber will be happy to have you home."

Jade stepped up on the side step, gave Amber a big smile, then she crawled into her booster seat, buckled herself in, and I handed her a juice box.

As I backed out of the parking lot my mind shifted back to the assistant teacher's comment. *Why had I taken someone else's word for it? Why didn't I even try to talk to the principal?*

When I pulled into our driveway, Randy followed us into the house. The purple passion rhodies flanking the porch were in full bloom. Sometimes I felt like I could stare at them forever. When I began to travel through the neighborhoods of Seattle, I was enchanted at almost every turn. Cherry tree blossoms. Red, yellow, and purple azaleas. Fuchsia hanging from porch baskets.

I opened the door. Jade and Randy went in ahead of me.

"I'll get you guys out in a few minutes," I called to Kiroc and Rocket as I went to put my purse in the bedroom. I set Amber in her baby walker and thought, *What have I done? It didn't even occur to me to look into the schools on the island. But then again, why would I? It wasn't like I needed anything special.*

I opened the doors to Kiroc and Rocket's cages, and they climbed up to the top. I took a few minutes to snuggle with them since Randy had stretched out on the couch.

Jade had gone to her room so I told him what happened with the assistant Kindergarten teacher. "One of the assistant teachers in Jade's class came out to talk to me in the parking lot. She said Jade doesn't belong there."

"Hmm."

"I don't know what we're supposed to do. It was Trey's wife, wasn't it, that told us she couldn't start Kindergarten until she was five?"

"There's that Christian school. It's mixed grade."

"What Christian school?"

"It opened last year. Seventh-day Adventist."

"I'm not sending Jade to a Christian school."

I went into the kitchen and put a mug of water in the microwave.

"You should at least talk to 'em."

Randy got up, downed a glass of water, and gave me a kiss. "I'm gonna mow the lawn."

Jade had wandered back into the living room. "Do you want some carrots? A blueberry muffin? I'm gonna have one."

"Muffin."

"I'll bring you some water, too."

I opened the fridge and pushed on the plastic covering the pork chops. They were still solid, so I put them on the counter. I washed my hands, finished fixing food, then hauled everything, and everyone, downstairs.

~ ~ ~

That night, I tossed and turned. When Randy said they had mixed grades, it threw me. If Jade was part of a mixed-grade class, hopefully we could figure out where she needed to be.

I'd attended a Christian school. The Jesuit University. I attended church when I was a kid. It didn't stop me from becoming someone who wanted to learn all I could, no matter which direction it took me. I believed that most of the people who attended church were good. They were doing their best to do what they believed was right, like Zola.

The next morning, when Randy got back from his morning walk, I said, "I've decided I'll at least take the time to check out the Christian school."

~ ~ ~

I was told I could come the next day.

A tall, dark-haired woman greeted me. I explained that I had attended church off and on all of my life, but had encountered some issues that had caused me difficulty.

She said, "We don't teach courses in religion. It's not part of the curriculum." She wasn't young, but she wasn't old, either. Her kind face expressed empathy. "All we do is spend an hour in the chapel each Friday. The kids can spend the time however they wish. It isn't directed."

I thought, *That doesn't sound bad.*

"We're different from the public school. We think education goes beyond a desk. We take lots of field trips."

I thought, *Jade would love that. She loves to be outdoors and active.*

The woman gave me a tour of the campus and explained that the activities included museum visits, boating excursions, and traveling to Bellingham to go ice skating. I thanked her for her time and told her we would see her in the fall.

## ~ N A N A I M O ~

A stout woman with her hair pulled back in French braids was sitting on our fireplace bench. She kept pushing herself into the corner next to the short wall on the dining room side as Randy discussed our upcoming summer sailing trip. He had been trying to find someone to help him take the boat to Lund for a couple of months. He said he'd go alone, but I was worried about his safety. Then he showed up with this woman.

"I can't go unless you can pay to fly me back," she said. "I need to get back quickly, and I can't pay for it."

I thought, *We can't, either.*

Randy mentioned that he'd been talking to the guy he bought the boat from, and he suggested meeting in Nanaimo. "Ceece can drive the truck to Nanaimo. Then you'll only have to take one ferry."

I had scanned the ferry schedule to Sidney a couple of times since we'd moved, at one point hoping we could go to some of the art exhibits in Victoria. A while later, I heard they made some changes to the schedule, but I figured there were just fewer sailings.

I said, "That sounds good," since it would mean a lot less driving.

The woman agreed.

~ ~ ~

The date for our trip approached, and I needed to make a reservation for the Sidney ferry. For a minute, I thought I was missing something. Then I realized it didn't stop at Orcas anymore.

The kids and I were going to have to take the ferry back to Anacortes, then get in line for the Sidney sailing. I couldn't complain to anyone.

~ ~ ~

The night before, as usual, I was pushed to my limit getting everything ready to go. I crawled into bed after midnight and the alarm rang at 5:00 a.m. As soon as I got up, I ran the truck down to the terminal to make sure we would get a spot.

I jog/walked the fifteen-minute distance back. The hill along the meadow was tough on good days, but I told myself it was good for me. I was going to be sitting all day. I got the girls up and dressed. I fed Rocket and Kiroc and told them that we would be back soon. Then we headed out.

By the time I got to the truck with Amber on my back, dragging our luggage and helping Jade keep up as she pulled hers along, I thought, *This is ridiculous.* I tried to switch my mindset, thinking, *It's okay. I'm going to have a couple of weeks off. I don't have to worry about missing a plane.*

After an hour-plus east and another hour-plus west, we passed the house. I tried to be thankful that the ferry rides gave us plenty of time to eat, and we didn't have to worry about stopping for restroom breaks. I was pretty sure we could make it all the way to Nanaimo after we disembarked. All I could think was, *When I get there, I'm going to be able to rest.*

The two-hour drive felt like eight. I pulled into the marina parking lot and looked for a place to park. Then I called Randy.

He told me where to meet him, and I couldn't understand why he wasn't coming up to help. I got the kids out, grabbed our luggage, and headed toward the docks. I could see him in the distance. As I approached, he started to yell.

"Oh, my God," he said, flailing his arms. "You're never going to believe what happened. That woman is insane! We need to leave now." He kept backing up in the direction of the boat. I looked at him in a state of confusion. Didn't she need my keys? Where was she?

"We have to go! You'll never believe what she did! This morning when I told her we needed to leave she dove off the boat and wouldn't come back!"

I thought, *Well, you made it on time, but okay.*

"She's crazy!"

*And now she's driving off with our truck.*

I didn't have the strength to argue. It didn't make sense, but I was practically delirious. When we got to the boat, Randy loaded our bags. He told Jade to watch Amber while he started to prepare to leave.

"I don't want to go anywhere. I'm too tired. Can't we stay here for the night?"

"We can't. She might come back."

I thought, *That woman has to be miles down the road by now. What is the problem?*

Randy started to untie the lines. A breeze was coming from the north. The boat was nose in, tied up on the port side. I stood on the dock and pushed off as Randy went to the wheel. As soon as he shifted into reverse, I hopped on.

The bow turned into the dock, so I grabbed the fending pole which we kept on top of the main cabin, and tried to push off. Then I dropped it into the water.

I hopped back onto the dock and struggled to reach it as it floated in between the boat and the dock, thinking, *I shouldn't have to be doing this.*

The boat kept moving closer toward the dock as I thought, *A boat can't crush an arm, can it?* I was finally able to grab the pole and hop back on. Randy powered back up. The rear end turned sharply away from the dock. Then we stopped. The anchor, which was hanging off the bow, was hooked on an electrical box.

*Oh my God,* I thought. *He's going to get us electrocuted.*

I ran up to the bow. Randy inched us forward as I used the fending pole to push against a dock piling. Then Randy applied enough power that the nose was finally able to clear the box and the end of the dock. I went below as Randy turned the boat and set his sights on Lasqueti Island.

~ ~ ~

I did my best to enjoy the trip, but I couldn't believe what had happened. Randy had never completely ignored me. He didn't seem to have any awareness of my condition, the level of exhaustion I was experiencing. My words didn't seem to even reach him.

As day after day went by, I couldn't get the rest I needed. Anchor chains clanked at odd times of the night. Swells hit the aft end with irregular thumps. Amber and Jade whimpered and turned in their sleep.

I was up and down the companionway stairs at least a hundred times a day taking care of something, like food spilling across the deck when we hit rough water rounding Sutil Point.

We visited some new places. We found calm water and walking opportunities along Rebecca Spit. I enjoyed the thrill of walking through a sand dollar breeding pool at Manson's Landing. The beauty of the waterfall and short hike to the freshwater lake at Teakerne Arm was stunning . But nothing about it was a vacation.

As we made our way home, I rationalized everything. We couldn't do anything else for vacation because finishing my projects might mean missing a plane flight. We didn't have money to pay for hotels, and why would we when we had our own personal floating one? The waters of the local sound were visible everywhere we could go locally, and Randy would spend all of his time thinking about being out there.

### ~ U N E X P E C T E D   G U E S T ~

When we got home I felt like I had rubber bands connecting me to everything– my desk, the kitchen, the kids, Randy. As I tried to function in one of the places, I could feel the pull of the others. Sometimes I was snapped back to a different one in an instant, completely unprepared for what I had to deal with.

Every weekend we either had company, I had something planned for the kids, or I was restocking and recouping. This weekend wasn't any different. It was Sunday, and company was arriving on the 4:25 p.m. sailing.

I sat down on the couch, trying to ignore the wear on the cushions, trying to ignore the fact that we'd had it 15 years, and put my feet up on the glass table. I needed a break. I didn't know where Randy met Brian and Jennifer. I couldn't remember if I had ever met them.

I looked out past the marina. There were ripples on the water. The ferry had arrived. Randy was picking them up at the terminal. A minute or so later, a dark clump of material fell on the deck in front of the sliding glass door. I figured a crow or squirrel was knocking pine needles or leaves out of the gutter. I got up to see what was going on, and a cockatiel landed in the middle of the deck.

I thought, *Oh my God. Someone lost their bird. I wonder if I can catch it.*

As I opened the slider, it flew to the top of the guard railing.
I took a couple of steps toward it, but it flew off toward the property next door.

I slid the door closed and called Jade. "Could you please come out and watch Amber for a few minutes?" Jade appeared in the hallway. "There's something going on with a bird outside. I'll be by the Cooper's house. Your father should be back any minute."

I grabbed a large towel, and as I opened the door, Jennifer was coming down the walkway.

She said, "You won't believe this, but when we got off the ferry and passed by the market, everyone was talking about this little bird. One of the guys was able to get it on his finger, but he couldn't catch it."

I said, "It's here. Come with me. That's why I have this towel."

I walked past her and she followed. I headed toward the neighbor's property on the west side of the house, looking for the bird, afraid that it had flown too high or too far.

The neighbor's yard was enclosed with a wooden fence. When I reached the meadow end and took a couple of steps onto their property, I could see the cockatiel sitting on the top of the fence railing.

"Take this towel and keep an eye on the bird. I'm going to grab another towel and go around, inside the fence."

I grabbed another towel, then ran up to the road, and made my way back along the inside of the fence on Cooper's property.

I stopped when I was about ten feet away and said to Jennifer, "Open the towel as wide as you can and walk toward the bird."

She took a couple of steps, and the bird flew my way, landing on the ground. I threw my towel over it and picked it up.

I couldn't believe that the bird that had been down at the ferry terminal just a few minutes before, had flown nearly a quarter of a mile east along the road, then when it reached the meadow, adjusted its path just enough to fly straight to our house. Not only that, it came to a house that already had birds, so we had the right kind of food.

~ ~ ~

This time I used the word miracle. The odds of that tiny bird making it all that way, in that amount of time, was insane.

Randy and Brian went out to the shop to build a make-shift cage out of chicken-wire and wood as Jade, Jennifer, and I processed the event by going over and over the details. When Randy brought the cage in, I put a container of water in the bottom and another filled with food.

Jade tried to help, lifting the water to the bird's beak and crushing nuts and seeds for it off and on throughout the evening. After we thought it had gotten enough to survive the night, I put a cover over the cage to let it rest.

## ~OUT OF THE SHADOWS~

Since Amber had been born, I was even more thankful that I worked from home. I was able to be with my kids when many women couldn't. I had a hard time making sense of it. Even with that, I had a hard time getting everything done I needed to do in a day. Exercise was usually last on my list even though I could get a pretty good walk, with the hills in the area, in about 30 minutes. Sometimes I took both girls, sometimes I strapped Amber to my back, and sometimes, I took the time to walk alone.

The roads on Orcas Island were narrow. The edges crumbled into gravel and dirt shoulders. I usually walked to the ferry terminal and back, but once in a while, I went the opposite direction. The two-mile loop was heavily forested, but roughly in the middle, there was a parcel of land tucked up against a cliff. A white two-story house with a large garden sat on the property and every so often I saw some of the family members tending the garden in long, black robes.

They never waved. They never even seemed to turn my way, but I hated the way I felt walking by whenever they were outside. I told myself there wasn't any reason to be uncomfortable, but where ever those feelings came from, they had a pretty solid grip.

Shortly after Amber was born, someone left a gift on the porch. A purple and white quilt with an Orca in the center. No one ever said anything about it, and I wondered if it had come from that family. They saw me walking with Jade, alone, then while I was pregnant, then walking with Amber on my back. They were the only people I could think of that saw me regularly that I didn't think would tell me. It made me feel terrible that I wasn't able to thank whoever it was, but over time, as I realized I'd never know, I recognized that it had a positive impact on how I felt about that family.

The walk around the ferry terminal headed into the sunset and sometimes to Zola's generous welcome. One evening the three of us headed that way as the sun hovered above the horizon just beyond the hill. We were enjoying a cornflower blue sky with wispy pink clouds, and had almost reached the post office, when I heard children's voices. Through the evening shadows, I was pretty sure I could see two girls with the owner of the house on the east side. She had a couple of goats, and they were all standing together near the driveway about 100 feet up the hill.

A short time later, I found out the girls weren't just visiting. Their family had moved in to the next house over. They looked like they could be near Jade's age. Maybe they could be friends. Then I remembered. Jade had changed schools.


~ S U N N Y ~


Jade named the cockatiel, Sunny. It would sit on Jade's hand, so she wanted to keep it, but I told her we needed to ask around to see if we could find its home. Since it was still summer, the only places I could ask about it was in stores and on the ferry, but no one seemed to know anything.

After a couple of weeks at the Christian school, Jade climbed into the truck and told me that the other girls were excluding her. Hiding behind their books to talk to each other. Telling her they were saving a swing for one of their friends. I felt like I couldn't win. While the staff was welcoming, why did I think the kids would be? They knew each other from church. They had probably grown up with each other. They didn't need anyone else in their circle.

I decided to go on some of the field trips so I could get to know the kids and their parents.

A couple of weeks later, I began to notice that I was having difficulty breathing when I was cleaning Sunny's cage. I knew, eventually, that it would impact the entire house. I didn't have any problem with the macaws and thought, *Why? Jade loves the little guy.* But I felt like I needed to renew my efforts to find its owner.

On one of the school field trips, I was sitting toward the front of the ferry and a woman sat in the seat next to me. It seemed unusual to me that anyone would sit so close. I said hello and asked her if she lived on the island. She said she was a snow bird, living on the island in the summer and in the southwest in the winter.

I told her the story of the cockatiel, that I was hoping I could find its home, but that it had been quite a while.

She said, "I live out White Beach Road. A woman who lived up there had cockatiels, but I think she gave them all away."

I said, "Is there any way you could find out if she lost a bird in August?"

"I don't think she's coming back," she said. "But her daughter lives on the island. I might be able to contact her."

It didn't sound like a sure thing, so all I could do was hope. We exchanged phone numbers, and I thanked her for her time.

~ ~ ~

It was election year. In mid-October, I picked Jade up from school and as she climbed into the truck she said, **"The boys are calling Al Gore a baby killer."**

She was six.

Then she said, "What's a faggot?"

As we wound our way home, I talked to Jade about pregnancy and the stages of the development of a fetus. I talked to her about religious beliefs, love, and freedom. I never dreamed anything like this would happen. My head was reeling, hoping Jade would understand, but knowing that was a lot to ask of a six-year-old.

I wondered who put those words into the boys' heads. Did it come from the news or from their parents?

I couldn't understand how any parent, no matter what their views were on abortion, could say that in front of their kids. I tried to imagine how those kids felt, thinking that there were people in the world who were killing children.

## ~MINDSPACE.20~

And I was one of them.

Someone who had an experience no boy or man ever would.

Their words carried so much weight.

My words—when I told my boyfriend that I'd forgotten to take my birth control for two days—didn't.

My words—when I told him that we shouldn't have sex that weekend—didn't.

His words—when he told me he would pull out—words I could hardly bring myself to repeat because somewhere along the way I learned that women "weren't allowed" to talk about those things—did.

Then I lay there in shock as he broke his word, violating my trust, while taking pleasure in it.

He tried to redirect my life for his benefit, so I would always be part of his.

I would have lost my education. The place I had earned in the graphic design program.

I carried the experience with me silently, knowing that every woman deserved the right to control her own life, her own body.

But given the "pro-life" arguments I heard over and over, I didn't think there would ever be anything that could change their minds.

## ~ C O M P L E X I T Y ~

A call came from the woman who had information about the cockatiels. She said she'd been able to connect with the woman's daughter. The daughter had one of the bird's siblings and was willing to take Sunny.

I asked if she could come to pick up Sunny when Jade was in school. I thought it would be too hard for Jade to see Sunny go. As I stood in the doorway I had second thoughts, wondering if Jade should have been there. There probably wasn't a good way to handle it.

~ ~ ~

My work continued to dwindle. It wasn't as steady as either Randy or I wanted. The industry was moving quickly to digital.

I bought software so I could start building websites, but the three-inch thick manual sat on my desktop for months. I read my way through parts of it like I had done with other software manuals, but by the time I found my first client, I had forgotten most of it.

I fought my way through the first website and found a few more businesses that were interested, but they seemed to think that converting files from print to digital would be as easy as flipping a switch. I couldn't charge them for all of the time I spent sitting there crying or screaming at the computer when I couldn't figure something out hour after hour, like how to move a line down.

In order to maintain my sanity, I decided to start attending the writing workshops at the library.

~ ~ ~

Whenever it was time for me to leave, Jade and Amber would often be at the dining room table having breakfast. All they had known for their entire lives was that mother was home. I felt like they would be spending the next couple of hours waiting for my return. I could see it in their eyes as I said goodbye, but I felt like it was time for them to realize Mom had a life of her own.

The group was mostly women. We'd listen to a speaker or a reading. Some people would share their work.

Every month I arrived with my sporty white, shiny binder, the vehicle I thought would steer me toward a life I'd begun to dream of, but no one seemed to want to look under the hood. They were willing to peek inside when I opened a door. Willing to listen to a story or two, but no one was willing to get inside and take a drive.

As each month came and went, the relationships remained distant. It began to feel more like I was carrying around an illegitimate child.

One morning, after setting down my two-inch thick binder, I saw Maya sitting at the end of the table. I wondered why she was there. Did Randy tell her? I spent the entire session thinking, *Should I stay pissed off or should I show her what I've been doing so she can understand at least that much?*

When the workshop was over, I picked up my hopes and dreams and stopped at the end of the table.

I said, "This is the reason I haven't been around much."

She said, "Why don't we go to my house and talk?"

We drove back to the house, and I told Randy and the girls that I was going to visit with Maya. I could feel the girls' disappointment, but I thought, *I need to be able to do this. Randy needs to take care of them once in a while.*

When we got to Maya's house, I flipped through the book. The space that seemed to have been containing me burst. Maya said she had a written a similar book, as well as a number of essays. She said she would share them and that she had tons of books I could borrow.

It felt like Maya was leading me into an underground cavern. One you can't see on the sun-scorched hillside. When you step into the entrance, the cool air gives you a chill, you hesitate for a moment, then it starts to feel good.

As you descend, you know you need a guide. Someone who knows where they are going. As you reach one plateau after another, millions of stalagmites and stalactites reach out like arms, from the drip, drip, drip of time. You want to connect with every one of them, but it can be dangerous if you stay too long.

Time had warped, collapsed. I was only there a couple of hours, but the intensity of the pull to go home had become too strong. We made plans to get together the next weekend.

I walked back along the narrow dirt road, hoping to feel the comfort of the towering trees. Instead, when I walked in the door, I felt like everyone could see complexity splattered all over me.

## ~ THE STARFISH ~

I was sure our next summer vacation was going to be better. Things were different. Jade was seven. Amber, nearly two. When I looked into the future, I expected things to improve. Sure, there would always be downturns. I didn't expect life to be perfect.

I knew what it took to drive up the coast to Lund and figured this time, the girls and I could do it ourselves. Jordan helped Randy get the boat to Lund. He planned to catch a seaplane from Refuge Cove back to Skyline, which was walking distance from the Anacortes ferry terminal.

The boat was tied up along one of the main floats when the girls and I arrived. Randy helped us unload our belongings, then he and the girls stayed in the day parking lot just above the boardwalk while I parked the truck in the upper one. When I got back, we took a walk along the boardwalk. I grabbed Amber's hand since the boardwalk had uneven boards and an occasional raised nail.

Along the way, we noticed a tiny, new souvenir shop. The display window couldn't have been much larger than a sliding glass door. They had a collection of glitter-bedizened starfish, and Jade wanted one. I pushed on the door and saw a note saying they were closed.

"We just got here," I said. "You're going to see lots of things in other places. If you don't see anything else you want, you can get one when we come back."

Jade was patient. She'd done enough shopping with me. The bright colors and sparkles were mesmerizing, so I knew she wouldn't forget them. We had dinner at The Boardwalk, and I hoped a Shirley Temple would help make up for it.

In the morning we headed north to Refuge Cove. We circled for a bit waiting for a place at the dock. Jordan helped us tie up. Jade, Amber and I climbed the rickety wooden steps up to the gift shop and store while Randy waited with Jordan at the seaplane pickup area.

After Jordan was gone, it only took about two hours to get to Gorge Harbor. We wanted to get there as early as possible to see if we could get a space on the dock. Even though it was expensive, it was nice for the kids.

Once we paid for the space at the harbor office, we walked the grounds and headed up a narrow, winding road. There wasn't much to see except a resident selling raspberries, but I was happy to be able to move around. At Refuge Cove, there was nowhere to go but the gift shop and store.

We ambled back to the docks and Jade took the lead. Then she screamed, "Look, starfish!" We hung our heads over the edge, and we could see down the pilings. There were hundreds of starfish and sea anemones. Pink, purple, gold, and green.

We found matching dresses for Jade and Amber and took pictures of them surrounded by wild roses and daisies before we had dinner at The Floathouse.

The next morning, we headed to Squirrel Cove. Randy wanted to explore the saltwater lagoon at the north end. The weather was cool, but not uncomfortable. The access to the lagoon was a challenge, but we made it in. We paddled around a couple of small islands, and I got out and circled one of them to get some exercise, but then I felt kind of ridiculous when I realized I probably looked like I was part of a caucus race like they had in *Alice in Wonderland*.

When we got back to the narrow passage to leave, the tide had gone out and there was hardly enough water to support the dinghy. Slippery sea algae covered the rocks at the entry, then, when we were all finally in the dinghy, we hit a large rock and everyone went tumbling. I was pissed at myself, and Randy because he knew more about the passageway than I did, for thinking we should be doing this with small children.

The next day we woke up to rain. Randy didn't say anything about a low-pressure system moving in. He had to have known it was coming. It turned out to be day-long, relentless drizzle. I told the girls we needed to be patient.

The rain continued the next morning, but Randy moved the boat anyway. The tides were well timed to get into Roscoe Bay, one of our favorite spots east of Black Lake. Randy thought that the turn of the weather might drive a few boaters away, and we would be able to get good moorage. I kept Randy's coffee hot as he shook drips off the hood of his gray slicker.

I put on a raincoat when we arrived and went to the bow to watch for the broad bridge of smooth stones that occluded the entry at low tide. We made safe passage and anchored. Randy tuned in to the marine weather reports on the VHF.

The rain continued the next day, and I wasn't willing to get off the boat with the kids. I did my best to keep them entertained, but their patience was wearing thin.

On the fourth day, it was still raining. We rotated sticker books, craft projects, and reading. We checked on the weather. More rain was expected.

On the fifth day, I was in tears. I was stuck looking out tiny windows that were positioned too high for the kids to see the horizon. Occasionally we went up on deck under the dodger, but it was cold and miserable.

On the sixth day, I cried off and on. The girls curled up beside me in bed, waiting.

On the seventh day, I mutinied.

"I want to go home," I cried. "I know I'm going to ruin everyone's vacation, but I can't do this anymore."

The next day we motored to Lund. The wind was blowing. The sea, ugly. I packed our belongings on the way, crying and apologizing to everyone. Feelings of guilt overwhelmed me. But there was something else I couldn't share that day. I was done with boating.

The boat was a huge expense. In most of our arguments, I brought up the idea of selling it. I wanted to switch to something small, trailer-able, so we weren't tied to it for every trip. Every time I brought it up, Randy told me we couldn't.

When we got to Lund, I ran our bags up to the truck thinking, *I don't care anymore. He can do what he wants. It doesn't work for me, and it doesn't work for the girls.*

Then I took Jade up to the souvenir shop so she could get a starfish.

It was closed. I thought, *Oh, my God. Not this.*

My apologies sounded weak as I curled her under my arm, but I had to keep moving forward. We needed to get food for the trip home, so we hurried over to the market. I stood at the deli counter, a refrigerated case about five feet tall with a glass face that sloped back at an angle, waiting to order meat and cheese.

Jade stood quietly beside me. Then she started pointing at something. The top of the case had scattered knick-knacks, jewelry stands, stuffed bears, seals, orcas, and overflowing seashell baskets. Jade was pointing to a pile that I was looking past as we were waiting for the salesperson. I turned my focus to it as I tried to figure out what had caught her attention when I realized there was a starfish in the middle of everything.

I hiked her up a bit to look at it.

"Those aren't for sale," I said. "They're just for display."

The salesperson was standing at the opposite end of the counter, but somehow she heard me and said, "No, they're for sale."

"How much?" I asked, always carrying the weight around of the saying, "If you have to ask, you can't afford it."

"Ten dollars."

I thought, *That's all?*

I'd never seen anything like it. It was as if the starfish I knew as a kid had morphed into a super-starfish, with extra-special starfish abilities. It had knobs that extended vertically almost two inches in the center, and some of the knobs had smaller knobs that grew out of the sides creating three-dimensional star-shaped arrays.

I couldn't believe that Jade had been able to see it. Only about an inch of one arm was sticking out over the edge of the counter. Then, I wasn't even going to ask if it was for sale. My mind was clearly muddled with everything that was happening, but Jade hadn't given up, and she got an incredible treasure.

As we walked back to the boat to get Amber, I couldn't help but think, *It seemed like that was supposed to happen. That she was supposed to find this special, natural treasure instead.*

But it was also hard for me to tell if Jade actually liked it. It wasn't neon and sparkly like the one she wanted. I didn't know if she knew that the bright colors and sparkles were fake, while this one had intrinsic beauty, so I did my best to explain it as the three of us headed back down the highway.

~ ~ ~

I sat on the master bed looking out at the marina. I didn't want to step onto a boat ever again.

I did laundry, spent some time with the birds, then I took the girls to visit my parents. They had moved to Issaquah because my youngest sister had moved to the area, and she also had two daughters. My parent's home was close to a large farm that offered entertainment for kids, so Jade and Amber got to ride a train, pet horses, and watch local performers in a play. It was dry and dusty. Everything felt small compared to the adventures we had on the water, but I told myself, *It's just different. You'll get used to it.*

We lived in vacation-land for lots of people. But I'd never hiked around Moran State Park, and we'd only gone to Cascade Lake a few times.

The girls and I began to attend local festivals and street fairs. A couple times a week, in the early evenings, I took them to the lake, which was at the base of Mount Constitution on the southwest side. I leaned against the logs lining the shoreline. It was hot, gritty, and noisy, but it was so relaxing to be able to sit there while the kids splashed in the water or played on the park equipment with kids from the island. I didn't have to do anything. I didn't have to think about anything. It was the first time in years that I felt rested.

## ~ S E A R R A E S ~

In the fall, when Jade went back to the Christian school, she knew everyone. Everyone knew her. It felt like she had finally made the transition. Amber and I joined the group on field trips to the Pacific Science Center, Seattle Children's Theatre, and ice-skating.

No matter what was going on in our lives, I watched Randy take personal time, stopping by to see Denny, Todd, or Kevin on his daily morning walk, driving over to have coffee with Steve and Tina (which Tina often shared with me later), so even though I usually felt like I was being irresponsible, I picked up the pace on my writing.

I'd work on graphics projects as they came, review and respond to emails for Randy, feed the birds and clean their cages, feed and care for Amber until she finally took a nap. Then I spent time on my writing. In the late afternoons or on weekends when I took the girls to the lake, to the park, or to ride bikes in the school parking lot, I kept a spiral notebook with me.

Nothing seemed to take away the guilt, but I tried to absolve myself by thinking about something my father said after he and my mother visited for one of Jade's birthdays. I was sitting near the fireplace, and I realized that I couldn't focus on anything.

My father must have realized I was struggling because a week or so later he said, "You've got to stop. You're killing yourself. If Randy wants all of those toys, let him pay for them himself."

I was sure we could fix things with a few changes. But Randy pushed back on everything. He always left completely unfazed, while had to lift myself up, again and again, out of the emotional wreck I kept getting buried in.

~ ~ ~

I could probably count on my fingers the number of times family members had come to visit. When they did, it felt like they drove past a huge span of my life without so much as a glance at the ways that I had grown, the accomplishments I'd achieved. As if they carried my past in their bags, unable to see me any differently than I'd been as a teen.

Jade kept telling me she wanted a dog, and after what happened with Sunny, I decided to get one. I felt like it would add to the girls' feeling that they had family. I wanted a small dog, like the dachshund our family had when

I was a young girl, but they barked a lot and the birds already made too much noise. Randy said he had always wanted a Borzoi, so I did some research and thought it would be a good choice. They were hearty dogs that could manage outside if needed, and they didn't bark.

We found one a short time later. A fluffy white cloud, with one brown patch on her head and one on her tail. Given my love of words, I created a palindrome that sounded the same as the name of cloud formations, Searraes.

## ~ H E E L S ~

I spent the late fall house training the dog, spending every day thinking, *Another fucking nightmare. But this, too, will be over soon.*

Jade was given a part in a school play, but problems arose everywhere. Since I had managed to live through a number of creepy incidents as a kid, I tried to not make too big of a deal of them. But what I experienced also wasn't targeted directly at me, so when I picked up Jade from school, and she said that one of the boys was kicking the back of her heels while she was trying to recite her parts, I talked to the teacher.

I was invited to sing with the choir. Once again I thought it would be helpful to be involved. It did show me one thing. That I should never try to sing in public even though some of my poems often ended up as songs.

~ ~ ~

On Valentine's Day, I dropped Jade off at school thinking about how much I enjoyed it as a kid. Getting candy at school and talking all day about the cards the other kids gave us.

My phone rang a couple of hours later. It was the school receptionist.

"Jade is really upset. Something happened with a couple of boys in her class. Can you please come as soon as you can?"

I put a coat on Amber and grabbed her day bag. I was so thankful I was home. As I cleared Uffda Hill, I looked at the speedometer. I was doing 50. I made myself slow down, but when I reached the parking lot, I quickly grabbed Amber and hustled into the building.

"I'll let Mrs. Maykine know you're here." The receptionist walked down the hall to my left. Within a minute or so, she and Mrs. Maykine appeared with Jade.

"A couple of the boys upset Jade in class. I think it would be best for her to go home."

"Okay. Thank you."

We got into the truck, and Jade told me what happened.

"Jeremy and Mark called me a liar."

Jeremy was the kid who had been kicking Jade's heels during play practice.

"Where was the teacher?"

"She left the room for a couple of minutes."

Jade was visibly shaken, but she continued, "They pushed me into a corner. They were screaming, 'You're a liar! You're a liar! You're not as good as you think you are.'"

~ ~ ~

When Randy got home, I said, "I'm going to handle this one."

I called the public school and explained everything to the principal, going back to what the Teacher's Assistant said to me when Jade was in kindergarten. I told her that Jade needed to move up to third grade. The principal said Jade would have to take a quiz and answer a few questions. We set up a date.

As I drove Jade to the public school, she looked out at the playground and said, "It looks safe here. There aren't any bushes."

As soon as I confirmed that Jade would be allowed to move up to third grade, I went back to the Christian school and asked to speak with Mrs. Maykine.

"The kids were left alone in the room," I said. "Why didn't anyone tell me?"

"I'm really sorry. It was just for a minute."

"Jade is going to move back to the public school. I'm going to need a document giving her permission to move to third grade."

"We can find a way to work things out. You won't need to pay for the rest of the school year."

I thought, *Oh my God. She's trying to buy me off.*

"No," I said. "I just want the paperwork."

Jade moved ahead of the kids she'd known in kindergarten. I didn't know how she was going to make any friends, but slowly things improved. Jade was allowed to skip the time period set aside for reading to take a French course a parent was offering. We also found out the school held violin classes a couple of days a week before school and Jade started to attend. We also met the girls down the road. One was in second. One was in fourth, but I was thankful Jade finally had some friends in the neighborhood.

A short time later, Randy told me he was going to Desolation in August, alone.

~ ~ ~

A month after Randy got back, I opened our credit card statement. My frustration and anger turned into depression and fury.

I continued to try to convince Randy to sell the boat. Instead, he took it out year-round with friends or strangers that he would occasionally bring home unannounced. Or he would spend the day hanging out at the boat to change the oil or install a new gadget. When he wasn't working on the house. Or building a new garage.

I didn't want a divorce. I was afraid it would hurt Jade and Amber. I wanted to be able to work things out.

Randy could always justify his spending. I didn't ever have any money.

I was sure that if we could just sell the boat, we could stabilize our financial situation.

Our arguments were now fights.

# CHAPTER TWO: THE PLANT

IN THE MINDSPACE OF SINGULARITY, we can only imagine one self, one consciousness.[26]

At an age where my perceptions still revolved primarily around me, a comment, which could have been any one of many, allowed my mind to shift from the singular "that isn't fair," (meaning it only applied to me), to the multiplicity of "life isn't fair," (meaning it applied to all of life). It was a step, a normal one, where I began to think in terms of a bigger picture, but I still accepted what I'd been told.

It took years for me to understand what all of it meant. Perhaps it took the split, of part of me into Jade, before I could truly see the multiplicity of consciousness. It had been appearing right in front of me, but I didn't think "I was allowed" to believe it. Over time, it became impossible to deny the things Jade said, the things she saw, and the things we saw together, as well as the things that happened when I was carrying Amber and as she grew from part of me and part of our shared ancestry.

There were times I could see the expansion of my consciousness into "our" consciousness. Given our physical connection, it made some sense, but it was breathtaking to see how far it could expand beyond that.

## ~ M I N D S P A C E . 1 8 ~

When I started college, I was asked to write a personal essay. The professor frowned at my paper, which I had titled, "We're Only Human." She said I needed to rethink what I had written, that it was too pessimistic. She said I was focused on limitations, instead of potential.

As if I believed I'd risen from a kind of biblical mud that slowly dried and solidified into a singular, unchanging object. But who at that age understands the pressures deep within the cycles of life? The cracks that can form in stone where soil could flow, where a seed could land and a flower, a bush, or a tree could grow?

And who would ever think that strangers--women buckled by time, backs bent from invisible weights, cracks and crevices in the landscapes of their faces--could know someone better than they knew themselves?

## ~ M I N D S P A C E . 2 2 ~

I had taken the bus to Seattle to get supplies for one of my design courses. There was always something on my list: layout boards, X-Acto blades, Prismacolor pencils.

On my way home, I took the seat at the very front, the wide single seat on the right.

An elderly woman came up the steps a couple of minutes later, so I stood up and offered the seat to her. Instead of walking toward the back so I could sit down again, I grabbed the overhead railing. After the woman sat down, she looked up at me and said, "Someday you're going to be a writer."

I smiled, thought about it for a minute, then dismissed it.

I'd read Tolstoy and Dostoyevsky. Writers knew the secrets of life, like doctors. They knew what made your heart race and your stomach churn. They understood how your family history affected your strengths. And they knew you'd probably have to cry a little before you'd feel better.

Still, more times than I could recall, as I experienced the incomparable beauty that was pouring forth in some of the books I was reading, I felt sick that I didn't have that kind of talent.

## ~ THE SPIRIT OF THE SEASON ~

I was screwing up. I needed to learn how to create websites. I was wasting my time with my writing.

An email notification arrived announcing the library workshop for December. The theme, "Celebrating the Season." I read it anyway.

"This workshop won't be limited to stories about the holidays. Feel free to bring anything. We hope to see you there!"

I couldn't do it. Everyone would bring Christmas stories anyway. I wasn't looking forward to the holidays, and I wasn't good at pretending.

*Why would anyone even show up when there were only two weeks until Christmas?* I thought. *Didn't people have last-minute shopping? Wouldn't they be traveling?* It seemed like it would be embarrassing to show up. To let anyone know I didn't have other priorities.

Still, I called Maya Friday night to see if she was going, but she was leaving in the morning on the red eye.

I hung up the phone thinking, *I don't want to go alone.*

I argued back, *You were going alone before Maya showed up.*

The arguing continued. *It's embarrassing. I should have other plans.*

*It's your time to meet with writers. It's important. You writing is important.*

*What would I take?*

*How about a couple of your poems?*

*They're not very good.*

*Your writing matters.*

I wasn't able to turn my mood around, but I talked myself into going. Or so I thought.

~ ~ ~

When I arrived, the building was dark. I thought, *Is it the wrong day? Oh, my God. I just wasted an hour coming into town. This is ridiculous. Why am I here? Well, I spent the fuel, I should at least go check the door.*

When I pulled on the door, it opened. I walked to the conference room and saw a couple of people. I realized I'd forgotten my water bottle, so I set my binder at the end of the table and went back to the truck.

When I came back in, a couple of people had taken seats, so I stood at the end trying to figure out where to sit.

I had only been standing there a minute or so, but I felt like I was going to implode. I couldn't decide. Finally I was able to convince myself that, while it wasn't appropriate for me to sit in the seat at the very front, right next to the workshop facilitator, I could sit in the second one.

A couple more people arrived and sat on the other side. The facilitator was about to get started when a woman appeared in the doorway.

She lived on the lower road in my neighborhood, so I knew her name, but I didn't know her well. She walked up the left side and took the seat right next to me. Right next to the facilitator. I thought, *Who does that at the last minute?*

Lauren and I said quick Hello's, and the director invited someone to start.

A woman on the opposite side of the table shared a story called "Camp was Our Cocoon" about a Christmas she spent as a child in a logging camp. Holed up in a shelter under twelve feet of snow, her parents used their imagination to craft ingenious, candle-powered toys. She ended her story by telling us that they had died recently.

Then a woman to the right of me read from a book she was writing about her travels. It revolved around the princess who inspired the Taj Mahal. The part she selected was about an encounter the princess had with a woman she had known when she was young.

I decided to be brave. I shared a poem called "Keeping up with Joan," about my current feelings, and a song called "Existential Highway," which I read in a way that I hoped would at least give everyone an idea of how it sounded.

One woman, Alice, who was sitting directly across the table from me, had driven up from Whidbey Island with her son, but neither of them brought anything to share, so Alice read someone else's poem.

I thought, *Why would anyone come this far without bringing anything?* Still, I enjoyed what she read.

There were so few people, we were done in about an hour.

~ ~ ~

We sat in an awkward silence, but no one made a move to leave. The meeting was scheduled for two hours, and all I could think was that everyone decided they were going to get what they came for: we didn't pay for it, of course, we were writers.

The facilitator asked if anyone had anything else they wanted to share. The woman to my right, who was working on the story about the princess, left us hanging so everyone said they'd like to hear more. When she finished, I shared a poem I'd written for Jade.

Then Lauren said she felt she was ready to share a story called "The Perfect Life" about a baby who had been born with a terminal illness. Family members had been informed about the situation and a number of them were able to make it to a nearby island to spend time with the baby. The child was held the entire three days of her life by people who loved her.

Again, at about 12:15 pm, we ran out of things to share. Still, no one got up to go.

~ ~ ~

The facilitator told us that her associate sent along a few poems we could read, if needed.

I sat there dumbfounded as everyone agreed. Sure, we'd all read more. I kept thinking, *Why isn't anyone leaving? Why don't these people have things they need to do? It is almost Christmas. Are we really just going to sit here and read random poems?*

The facilitator put the poems on the table upside down, then pushed the pile toward the center so everyone was within comfortable reach. Then she asked Lauren to start. Lauren read a poem called "The Hands."

Then the facilitator nodded at me. Mine was short and kind of silly, but I found myself thinking, *That's interesting, it's about kids.*

I was kind of tuned out, thinking about the poem I read, but then I heard the woman next to me say "palace." I listened carefully to the ending, "Both women have begun to cry, but neither stops her song."

At this point the pattern was set, the path was moving counter-clockwise. The next person in the circle, the woman who had shared her childhood story about spending Christmas under twelve feet of snow, started to read the fourth poem. It was called "Encounter." Word after word caught my attention: "...frozen fields at dawn...wonder...that was long ago...today, neither one of them is alive."

~ ~ ~

I interrupted everyone when she finished and said, "Did anyone else notice what just happened? The poems three of us read relate, almost directly, to what we shared today."

I couldn't remember what Lauren read. At that point, I thought the connections started with mine. I looked across the table and said to Alice, "But you didn't bring anything. Let's see what you've got."

She started to read, "...cries for the north it hopes it can find..." She was the one who had come up from Whidbey Island. When she reached the fourth stanza, the connection was clear:

"You come...and wait to hear it. You sit a long time, quiet, under the thick pines, in the silence that follows, as though it were your own twilight. As though it were your own vanishing song."[27]

Everyone nodded and agreed that it was amazing. Then we all started to collect our things. I was disoriented, trying to figure out if the first poem related to Lauren's work. The facilitator was standing at the end of the table organizing the poems. As everyone left, I said, "I can't remember now. Did Lauren's poem connect with her work?" The facilitator didn't look up, so I said, "Well, you know, she does a lot of work with her hands."

The facilitator nodded, but didn't offer any indication she wanted to discuss it any further.

On the way home, I stopped by the grocery store in Eastsound. Then as I drove down Horseshoe Highway, I thought, *Oh, my God. The hands. They held the child.*

I called the facilitator and asked if I could get a copy of the last set of poems. When I picked them up, I sat in the truck and read the one about the hands again.

"The poor hands, overworked and dry, dressing the body like maids. The poor palms with their geography of lines. One is broken, another tells us, short life."[28]

~ ~ ~

Lauren had to be sitting in that chair. I had to be sitting in mine.

Everyone did.

Four poems aligned perfectly with the work four people brought to read. One of the poems literally said, "You didn't bring anything, but you were waiting to hear something important. Here it is: You sat there in silence. That was what you were supposed to do and now you can see that there can be incredible beauty just because you showed up."

The feelings I had as I struggled with the decision about where to sit were intense. Then I couldn't believe Lauren could sit at the very front even though she arrived at the last minute.

But there was more.

Someone who didn't have a connection to any of us, who didn't have any idea what we were bringing, chose random poems she didn't even know we would read. I wanted to talk to the facilitator more about it, but I wasn't sure I should. Her body language was clear. She was definitely uncomfortable.

~ ~ ~

And there was more.

The arguments that happened in my mind the night before. Something kept driving me to come up with some reason, any reason, to justify going.

I'd been struggling with thoughts about my abilities as a writer, whether or not I'd ever accomplish anything, whether or not I was being negligent by spending so much time on it. I was worried that I wasn't going to be bringing the "right" kind of material, but as I drove home, I realized I didn't need to bring a holiday story. It was just the opposite. I had been given one.

~ ~ ~

My perspective shifted dramatically.

It had been four years since the event occurred with the fossil. Long enough that I didn't think anything else was going to happen. There was no question that I was experiencing something miraculous.

The odds were astronomical, but odds didn't even apply to what had been happening in my mind. Or the fact that the events connected to me in deeply meaningful ways about specific aspects of myself.

Sure, if everything connected to a carrot, I'd feel differently, but this was about a decision "made" to value my writing.

Six other people were involved.

I started to wonder if *everything* I'd been taught about God was wrong. Was the Creator actually trying to let me know that S/He supported me and my writing?

~ ~ ~

Both events, the one with the fossil and the one at the library, involved intense mental activity that affected me before they occurred. They weren't identical, but they were similar.

I began to think of questions I never dreamed I'd be asking, Is God actually communicating with me? Is it possible that God is really there for us?

I wanted to research and write every minute, but I couldn't.

Questions piled up upon questions.

Was I the only one? Did other people know about this? How could I find them? How much time should I be spending on my writing?

# SEEDS

I STOOD AT THE TOP OF THE STAIRCASE, bent over at the waist, trying to project the anger that was exploding out of me as far as I could.

Then I stopped.

Death was hovering in the energy in front of me.

"You're trying to kill me."

When Randy and I met, he told me that one of his family member died from a brain aneurysm. My head was pounding. I stood there wondering if anger, welling up from decades of duplicity, had caused it.

Randy stared at the ground.

It was embarrassing. Everyone in the neighborhood knew. Every couple of weeks Randy and I would "talk," then Randy would get up and walk out, saying he was going to have lunch with a friend, while I either yelled out the front door after him or was left in tears.

I thought my efforts would change things for the better, that I could bear the anger. I didn't think our children should have to cope with divorce.

One afternoon I sat in our living room looking out over the meadow, tied to the phone, wailing to one of my sisters. "I don't understand what you're complaining about," she said. "You have a beautiful home. A gorgeous boat. You're self-employed. Home with your kids."

~ ~ ~

My reading journey had moved from family issues, to relationships, to women's issues. When I was in the library one day, I looked to the right of the section on "motherhood" and noticed a section on "feminism." I took copious notes from book after book, hoping the answer to my marital problems would appear in front of me like one of the poetic sayings from a fortune telling machine.

Instead I found questions like, "Do you feel safe enough to express your feelings?" Or I was simply told that "literally millions of people suffer the effects of real or perceived isolation."[29]

It took more than fifteen books to find a couple of the words I needed to hear: emotional violence.

I didn't know it existed. I thought domestic violence was physical. "The violent partner will most likely apologize after hurting you."[30]

When Randy came home, he seemed to just push a button and reel off an automatic apology, while I stood there having to accept it because no one "should go to bed angry." Which I began to realize meant, so I wouldn't be mad enough the next morning to refuse to have sex with him.

During the summer, Kevin invited us to his house a few times for dinner. Kimberly left him not long before, and he wanted the women he was dating to know he was one of the good guys. During a conversation with one of the women, as we were watching the sun set from his balcony, she said that she was divorced and had a daughter. She owned a business as well, and asked about getting help with some brochures, so we exchanged phone numbers.

For the next couple of weeks, I wanted to call and ask her how she did it, how she made the decision to walk away, but I was afraid I would be imposing. She only gave me her number for business.

After days of telling myself it wasn't appropriate, but knowing there wasn't anyone else I could ask, I sat on the master bed and dialed her number. I told her I was stuck, that I wanted to see if she would be willing to tell me how she finally made the decision.

Her answer surprised me. She said she'd struggled with the decision because of her daughter, but a friend recommended Mira Kirshenbaum's book, *Too Good to Leave, Too Bad to Stay.*

I immediately ordered a copy. Each chapter described a problem that could occur in a marriage. Then at the end of each one, there was a question that allowed the reader to consider what they would do if the same thing happened in their marriage, if it would make them want to leave or stay. I answered 31 out of 36 questions: Leave.

Still, I couldn't walk away. We lived on an island. My business had been declining for years. I couldn't leave the birds. I couldn't leave Searraes.

It did finally make me realize one thing: how stupid I was being for wasting everyone's time.

~ ~ ~

Late one August afternoon, Randy was sitting in one of the black leather chairs in front of the sliding glass doors, and the conversation shifted to our financial situation. It didn't sound like an accusation when he said, "You made $30,000 last year," but I had earned a lot more in previous years.

I stood by the new range top, one of my birthday presents, thinking the conversation wasn't going any farther, when suddenly I said, "It's over."

As soon as the words slipped past my lips, I thought, *What have I done?*

Randy responded like he'd been expecting it and said, "When are you gonna leave?"

It felt like a spotlight had been turned on me. I couldn't speak.

Within a few seconds, I realized I had a life raft, an unintended gift from Randy.

Shortly after we got married, he told me that when his first wife decided to end their marriage, she stayed in their house until she could figure things out. I realized I had information every woman should know: some women run out of the house with a suitcase; some don't.

"The kids just started school," I said. "I'm going to wait until next summer."

I walked away in a daze. Thankful an answer came, but even with all of that time to prepare, it felt like I was looking into a deep, dark hole.

~ ~ ~

I decided not to join Randy in any more "talks." It didn't take long before I was experiencing an unusual state of calm. Whenever Randy came into the house, I acted like everything was fine.

I began to pack a few things in September, October, November, while thinking, *Why am I doing this? I can't pack enough right now for it to matter.* But I felt like I had to do something. As I tried to plan, I knew I had to be selective. I wasn't going to have much space. *Could I rent a moving van on the island? How was I going to move anything but boxes?* I was living in a constant state of uncertainty. *Would I come home one day to find the locks on the house had been changed? Did I need to buy a gun if I was going to be living alone with two small children?* I packed my books into double strength paper bags, wondering, *Will I have enough room for all of them?* I loaded shoe boxes with family keepsakes and tucked them into the back of bedroom closets that Randy and I had planned to convert to hallway storage, after he remodeled the master bath.

Day after day I passed a fireplace that had never seen a spark. Sometimes I stood at our bedroom window taking in the view of the lake and marina at the base of the meadow, saying goodbye to my dream as I ran my hand over the clear cedar wall covering.

## ~THE REHEARSAL~

I'd been helping Randy with his business for years so I continued. We both knew what we needed to do to keep things going.

Just before the holidays, Randy suggested trading in our crew cab Dodge Ram for two base models. I couldn't argue. When we arrived at the dealership I watched as he applied the value of the trade-in to his purchase. He got a four-wheel drive. I got a standard.

I expected the holidays to be challenging for Jade and Amber, but I also thought it would provide a kind of dress rehearsal for the change coming the next summer. Randy and I arranged separate visits with our families, and he took the girls to his parent's house first. I thought it would be nice to have a little time alone with my family, so I left at the same time they did.

I pulled into the driveway of my parent's two-story home due east of Kent. My father directed me to a room to the left, then he went upstairs. I set down my luggage, hung up my coat in the closet, and sat down in one of the wingback armchairs in the living room. My mother was sitting at the dining room table working on needlepoint. We were about as far away as we could get from one another.

I tried to start some small talk saying I was going to rest a few minutes then go to the mall for a couple of hours.

My mother looked up, her eyes narrowed in a manner I'd never seen before, and said, "Why aren't you with your husband?"

I said, "I told you guys we separated in August."

My father appeared by the railing in the upstairs hallway. He came down and sat about three feet away from me on a footstool and said, "You are going to destroy your children's lives."

From my conversations with Maya, I was able to parse the sentences into sections that allowed me to detach from the emotional aspects. I was able to separate myself from the intended impact, the emotional bomb, just by the fact that he used, "You are..." at the beginning of the sentence. Maya had explained that using "I" statements created less conflict. In one little way after another, I felt like I was getting better at defending myself.

I replied to both comments while managing to hold the pieces of myself together, patiently explaining my decision again. They didn't have any idea of the level of anger I had about the way Randy had been treating me, that I had finally realized how harmful it was, and that it wasn't okay for Jade and Amber to see me that way. I also didn't have the strength to explain that part of my decision to leave Randy had been made out of self-preservation, and I was going to have to do it again. I didn't allow myself to think about the amount of trouble I was going to be in as I grabbed my bag and headed to the door.

"What are we going to do with the gifts?" my father called after me.

"Give them to charity," I said as I rushed down the porch steps.

I couldn't think about anyone's shattered expectations as I sped up the freeway. I didn't want to talk to anyone about anything. When I got home, I crawled into bed and shut out the world.

For the next couple of days, I stayed in the master bedroom. When Randy got home with the girls, I knew Amber and Jade were confused, but they seemed to understand I needed space. My father had called Randy, so he stopped by and picked up the gifts. He helped Randy "save the day."

~ ~ ~

Over the next few days, I felt like a stranger to Jade and Amber. I felt like I'd betrayed them. I continued to rest, lying on the bed, wishing things could be different.

One afternoon in late December as I was walking into the bedroom, trying to process the fact that I didn't have any support, that I was probably screwing everything up, a thought occurred to me that was so strong it felt like I'd received an urgent message:

*We couldn't wait until summer. We had to move before the end of the school year.*

Jade was in sixth grade and still spent most of her time with the boys. I suddenly realized she couldn't walk into middle school alone the next fall. Amber had only attended part-time kindergarten. It would be just as traumatic. My quiet, five-year-old would be facing a full-time schedule without knowing anyone.

The questions about how I was going to make the move evaporated. I responded to the need to leave, as I now saw it, as if it were a directive.

~ ~ ~

I had been doing what I could. Saving a little money each month. Starting to think about our options. I dreamed about moving to Seattle, but visitation rights made it impossible. I wanted to get Jade into an advanced program Maya told me they had in Anacortes, but I knew I had to be realistic. Mount Vernon was the next-best option.

Then I realized I was giving up without trying, so I checked out rental rates on a few apartments. To my surprise I saw a couple of possibilities. I called the school district office to find out the best time for the girls to start. The receptionist said it would be right after Spring Break, the second week of March.

A couple of days later, as Randy and I crossed paths, once again words unexpectedly flowed out, "My plans have changed. We're going to move at the end of February."

To my surprise, Randy said, "Okay. We'll refinance the house and make a down payment on one in Anacortes."

"Okay," I said, trying not to sound stunned.

He added, "I looked up information on child support. I've got that all figured out."

Over the next few weeks, I tried to act like everything was normal, but Randy had taken control. I felt like a child watching a piece of candy in an outstretched hand, waiting for it to close.

## ~INTO THE NIGHT~

As we sat in the mortgage office signing paperwork for funds for the down payment, I watched the process carefully, buttressing myself in case there was some kind of trick, some kind of crack in the process that might cause it to collapse.

One of Randy's friends knew a woman who was selling her house in Old Town Anacortes. I wanted to make the most of the trip, so I called a realtor to see what else was available. I wasn't impressed with any of them, but I also didn't think I could be that picky.

The following Sunday, Randy left the island to run some errands. While he was driving through Anacortes, he noticed a listing on one of the Real Estate office reader boards. I was told that houses were selling fast so I made an appointment for the next day.

That morning it was my turn to deliver snacks to Amber's kindergarten class, so I drove down to the local market. When I walked in, a song was playing that I hadn't heard in years. I first heard it when I was in my teens and also heard it once, early in my marriage, as I drove away from a counseling session. I felt like it was playing for me, even though it felt stupid to think such a thing.

I was standing by the fruits and vegetables, wishing there was some way I could find out the name of the song, but also sure it wasn't going to happen when a man approached with a baby. I thought, *Just ask. Who cares?*

"No," he said, "Is it a classic?"

I explained that it had been years since I'd heard it, and I'd forgotten the name.

He said, "You know, some of these places have music piped in, and the song name is displayed."

I thanked the guy and ran to the front counter. At first the cashier said, "No," then he said, "Well, maybe." I followed him to the store manager's office, and there it was: "Into the Night" by Benny Mardones.

If I could fly

I'd pick you up,

I'd take you into the night

And show you love

Like you've never seen, ever seen…

All I could think was, *It's playing for me*, no matter how stupid it seemed. I sang the chorus over and over as I drove home.

~ ~ ~

The mother of the two girls who lived near the post office was willing to pick up Amber and Jade after school and watch them until Randy got home. He was driving back Monday morning, so he walked through the house before I got there. He called and said with the garage and curbed sidewalks, it would be a good investment. After I had a chance to see it, I told the realtor we were interested. She started to prepare the paperwork, then she said she'd received information that two other people would be bidding. A few minutes later she called back to say one of them dropped out.

The realtor and I went through the bidding process. At around 8:00 p.m. I put in a final bid, then I hustled to catch the 8:35 pm sailing.

For days, I had been reading the newspaper at dinner time to detract from the lack of conversation. I justified it by sharing some of the stories with the girls. Tuesday evening, as we waited for the call from the realtor, I opened the paper to Dave Barry's column and noticed the horoscopes near the bottom of the page. I didn't usually read them, but that evening something felt different. I thought, *What the hell? See what it says.*

Cancer for Jan 25th through 31st:

*Good grief, as if you're not already burning the candle at both ends, now we have the Full Moon in your sector of money and resources. What is it you need? You're gonna get it! But only if you actually open your mouth and tell people you need it! Oh, and there is the detail of needing to leave your house to talk to those people, too! This is your Moon to set yourself up to thrive. Get going!*

At nine o'clock we got the call. The house was ours.

~ ~ ~

On the first weekend of March, we left the island with two loaded trucks. I couldn't think about everything that was happening. I just had to keep moving forward.

A little over an hour later, I was in a new house, in a new town, with my kids in a new school, and my marriage was officially over.

Things didn't turn out perfectly. Jade couldn't get into the advanced program until the fall, but I was thankful for what I'd accomplished.

As I was unpacking, I remembered that the girls needed to see the new school before they started classes, and I hadn't scheduled an appointment. It was only three days away.

I couldn't understand why my mind did this. If the thought was there all along, why did it wait until the last minute?

## ~DIVINELY DIRECTED~

Monday morning I called the school to arrange a tour, hoping we could do it that afternoon, but the only spot the principal had available was Tuesday at 2:00 p.m.

When we arrived, after brief introductions, the principal gestured toward a set of double doors on the opposite side of the main entry. "This is our theater. Our pride and joy. We produce two annual plays," he said, as he headed that way. We walked up to it and peered inside. There was a large open area and a stage at the far right.

The principal motioned for us to follow him down one of the corridors and started to say something else, but at the exact same time an announcement blared over the loudspeakers. All I could hear was "...auditions this week!"

The principal proceeded as if nothing had happened and continued down the expansive hallway. "We also use the facility for other events throughout...."

"...spring play, 'Frog and Toad!'"

"…to the right is the science room. And the media lab is up ahead," the principal said, as we walked past a room with large vertical windows. "There's a computer for every child."

"...day after school!"

"And here is the library."

We turned around and headed back to the main office. The principal filled in a few more details as my mind leaped back and forth between our conversation and the information about the auditions. I was pretty sure I heard Thursday.

Jade loved acting. She'd performed in a number of plays with the island theater, including "Alice in Wonderland" and "North Pacific" (a parody of "South Pacific"). But by the time we said goodbye to the principal, I felt like I was being ridiculous. What kid would want to audition for a play after being at a school for two days?

Wednesday and Thursday flew by. I was trying to work while organizing everything else, but on Friday I was back at the school a little before noon providing some more paperwork.

As I stood in front of the receptionist's desk, I remembered the announcement. I was 99% sure the auditions were over and 99% sure Jade wouldn't be willing to audition, but I still asked the question.

The receptionist said, "Yeah. They held them yesterday."

For some reason my mind proceeded as if there was still a reason to continue. I yammered on saying, "Dang. My daughter loves acting. I've been so busy. I completely forgot about it."

I stood there thinking, *What am I doing? There's no reason to continue the conversation.*

The receptionist replied, "A couple of other kids missed it, so the school counselor is going to let them audition today at noon. I don't see why she couldn't, too."

I couldn't believe what I was hearing. I thought, *Oh, my God. The opportunity is still there. But I haven't even mentioned it to Jade.*

I made a decision for Jade based on an assumption, and suddenly I felt like it was important for Jade to make her own.

"Can I go to Jade's classroom to talk to her about it?"

The receptionist nodded and gave me an application form. I hurried down the hallway and knocked on the classroom door. I quickly explained the situation, and Jade said she wanted to give it a try.

~ ~ ~

Jade was seesawing. Up on the day she was told she had a lead part in the play, down on days she told me she was being kicked in the halls and pushed around on the playground.

I was volunteering in Amber's classroom, helping her with the transition, afraid day after day that Jade was going to have to spend the next three months that way. Even with all of my efforts, it looked like she was still going to be facing a difficult situation in the fall.

Then one afternoon, Jade told me that a couple of kids were talking with her during recess. They were kids from the advanced program that were also in the play.

Around the same time, at one of the rehearsals, the school counselor told me that he had been frustrated during the first set of auditions because he hadn't found anyone that could fill one of the leads, the part of Badger, but when Jade auditioned, he knew she was perfect for it.

Jade had never been given a lead part in one of the island theater's productions. She'd been hoping for that kind of opportunity.

~ ~ ~

The night before the final performance Jade was sick. It kept us up into the early morning hours, so she was still sleeping at four the next day. I called the counselor and explained the situation. He told me that he could fill in if needed, but he really didn't want to. I let Jade sleep as long as I could, and when I woke her up, she said she felt good enough to go. I let the counselor know we were coming, and she performed flawlessly.

~ ~ ~

I couldn't help but recall the "thought" I had in December. How it had pushed me with a kind of force I'd never experienced before.

Then there was the jolt I'd gotten when I was unpacking, when I realized that we needed to tour the school.

We had to move that week. We had to be at the school on Tuesday to hear the announcement.

I'd heard about premonitions, but I didn't think they were real. I couldn't believe how the timing worked out.

Jade was making friends, connecting with a few kids through the play that were also in the Challenge Program. That was the direction of the "thought" I had in December.

I was certain that Jade had been given a gift. It was wrapped up so neatly and suited her so perfectly, it should have also taken a bow.

## ~GUT PUNCH~

I shuffled through some of my business files and noticed a Social Security statement. I hadn't looked at one for a while, so I opened it.

My income the previous year: $7,000.

It felt like I had reached the moon while still being dependent on my ex to send oxygen tanks.

I was and I wasn't ignorant about our financial situation. I had been responsible for making sure the bills were paid each month. I balanced four checkbooks. I entered hundreds, if not thousands, of receipts for our tax records while Randy coordinated with the accountant. I thought I was doing enough. When I saw the numbers on the IRS forms, I looked at the total and signed it.

~ ~ ~

I felt like I had completely lost my moorings, but at the same time, I was tethered to something that was carrying me, us. The closest word I could find was that everything I was experiencing was somehow related to destiny.

But it didn't resemble destiny in the way I thought it was defined. Like how a child is destined to sing because they'd started when they were five.

Did everything have to be exactly the way it was the moment I walked away from Randy? Did I have all of the knowledge I needed at that moment? Like, if I had more or less knowledge, would that have stopped me from leaving when I needed to?

I was certain I was supposed to be in "that chair" at the library. Now it seemed like I was supposed to walk into the elementary school on that day at that specific time. Five minutes earlier or later, and we would have missed the announcement.

~ B I N G O ~

Since Amber was only five, Randy seemed to understand that it would be hard for her to spend a lot of time at the Orcas house the first summer. We started with every other weekend.

One afternoon in July, I was working in the front yard, crawling over the river rock, weeding, because I didn't want to use herbicides, and suddenly I remembered that there was a festival for kids happening that day. Once again, I was kicking myself thinking, *Why? Why couldn't I remember three hours ago?*

I ran the birds into the house then went upstairs to tell the girls, apologizing, but reminding them that we still had a couple of hours. It was just after three. We got ready as quickly as we could and drove to the park.

As we walked up to one of the tents, I could see that they were tearing it down.

"Oh, no," I said to Amber. "I'm sorry. It looks like the horses are going home."

Amber didn't respond. It was always hard to get her to say much. We walked through the grass to the other side where we could see more activity. I noticed a group to the left sitting on bleachers. Then I heard a call for a round of Bingo.

I glanced at the prize. A backpack. It wasn't something we needed, but I thought, *I don't know if the girls would have any interest in playing Bingo, but we can come back in a bit. If they're still playing, great. If not, no big deal.* We found face painting and a fish pond. The library was giving away books. The girls got snocones. We sat down and watched the crowd.

On the other side of the park, they were letting the air out of the blow-up slide. We wandered over that way and found a craft project the girls could do, but it didn't take long.

We went over to the Bingo bleachers and waited for the next round, while I sat there feeling like a terrible mother. We played a couple of rounds. Of course, not winning anything. Then they announced over the loudspeakers, "Last round! Blackout Bingo! Who's gonna play?"

I said, "Do you guys want to stay?"

They didn't seem to be all that interested. I looked at the prize: a go-cart. I thought, *What's the point? We're not going to win.* Jade was standing, taking a few steps toward the boxes filled with cards, so I said, "Jade, do you want to go get new cards?"

Jade grabbed Amber's hand and took her along. Amber chose two and handed one to me when she got back to her seat.

The guy in charge made the announcement over the loudspeakers a couple more times and the crowd grew. By that point there was nothing else to do. When the bleachers were close to being full, he started calling the numbers.

Amber was sitting between me and Jade so we could make sure she was getting her spaces filled. I was surprised to see how many all three of us were getting. With four or five spaces left we kept getting numbers. My heart started to race.

I thought, *You're being silly. We're not going to win.*

Another one was filled for all of us. Then another.

Each one of us had one space left. But they were all different numbers. Then Amber's number was called.

I couldn't believe it. I croaked out, "BINGO!" for her.

She didn't seem to understand what was happening as we made our way down with her card and they verified the numbers.

The crowd started to disperse. I wondered if they thought, *Who are those strangers who just won the go-cart?*

The announcer asked where we were parked, and I pointed to the space along the side of the road. He offered to help us with it, and we loaded it into the bed of the truck.

~ ~ ~

We'd just received another unbelievable gift. This time during the month of Amber's birthday.

It was so hard to process.

Was I supposed to ignore the fact that I just happened to remember the kid's fair at the last minute, and in another seemingly miraculous event, Amber won a go-cart? If I'd remembered earlier, would we have stayed to the end and played Bingo? I kind of doubted it.

My business associate, Rebecca, was one of the few people who stuck it out with me. She continued to send me work as she moved from one position to another. I continued to share my stories and she said, "You should send this to *Reader's Digest.*"

I thought, *Who's going to care about a little girl winning at Bingo?* And it wasn't the focus of my writing. I was pretty sure people who wanted to read about children didn't want to find out that the author's focus was sex, drugs, and challenging belief systems. I wasn't even sure if Rebecca would continue to stick around once she found out.

## ~VIGILANCE~

Since one of Randy's friends lived on the other side of town, I initially thought, *The move will be okay. We know someone who lives there.* But once I arrived, my perspective changed. Randy's friend wasn't someone I could turn to. Randy was now my ex.

I'd managed to hold on to a couple of the friendships I had on the island, for a while. My relationship with Tina was one of them. I could never thank her enough for sharing *Daughters of Copper Woman.* She also helped me when I was looking at houses. When I mentioned that one of them was in "Old Town," she asked about the address.

"You don't want to buy that," she said. "I know someone who lives in the area. She told me that there is a guy up the street who is a registered sex offender."

That didn't even occur to me.

After I got settled, I went to the police station and asked if they had pictures of local sex offenders. They handed me a book, and I looked through the pictures. It seemed like it would be impossible to remember the faces, so I made a list of names.

~ ~ ~

Shortly after Amber started first grade, she and I were at the library, and I saw a woman who had a daughter that was in Amber's class. As we passed by one another, I said hello, and we talked for a few minutes. I thought, *The library has to be one of the safest places to meet someone.*

Amber started playing with the girl. We invited her over to our house, and her mother invited Amber to theirs.

One afternoon the following spring, Amber and I saw them at a festival with a guy the woman introduced as her boyfriend. They were carrying some heavy items, and I was near my car so I asked them if they needed a ride. They accepted the offer.

That evening, as I lay in bed trying to fall asleep, my mind offered up the connection to one of the men's faces at the police station. I wanted to be sure, so I went back to check.

Then I asked if I could talk to a police officer. I told him what had happened, that one of the men in the registry was living with a woman who had a six- or seven-year-old daughter. He told me that they had talked to her a number of times and there wasn't anything more they could do. I mentioned that it was going to really difficult for Amber to stop seeing the girl, but I felt we had to. He said something about summer break coming, that maybe that would help us create some distance. I mentioned that Amber had been accepted in the program for highly motivated students the next year.

He said, "That will help."

~ ~ ~

I had walked away from people so many times in my life, and it seemed to be getting harder, not easier.

When I was a child, I walked away from a relationship without even being aware of it. Since that time, I've learned that I'm introverted, that it wasn't my fault. I was a couple of grades ahead of the girl. She had been my friend since we had moved into that house. When I met Naomi, the Mormon girl who lived at the end of the street, I can't remember seeing the little girl again. Then I walked away from Naomi. In that situation, I was aware of what I was doing.

I don't know if that was a turning point for me, but I wasn't long before I started to consciously walk away from people who didn't share my beliefs, who didn't follow the same set of rules.

I tried to connect with one person after another. Then I realized that even though we were in the same social group, which I thought meant we had at least something in common, I had to walk away.

That included most of my high school friends. People in college. People I had gotten to know in my marriage.

For a long time, I wondered why I had to be on that kind of path. But now I could see that some of those steps brought me to Sucia Island and Anacortes. Some of the steps pushed me to write about my life. And some of the steps brought Jade and Amber to a place where their abilities were being recognized.

But at the same time, I had to walk away from another little girl.

~ ~ ~

Summer break was coming. Randy sent an email telling me he wanted to flip the schedule we had the previous summer—the girls would live with him and see me every other weekend.

I asked Amber and Jade if that's what they wanted to do. They said, "No."

By this time, my father knew I had gotten the Jade and Amber into the Challenge program, and he helped me get an attorney. We met with a woman who said, "I know guys like this. We should be able to get a parenting plan done for $X." My father and I had lunch at a nearby restaurant and decided to work with her.

Four months later, the money was gone, and nothing had been done. The attorney would provide paperwork, and I would go through it and respond, but she kept telling me I needed to come in to the office to review everything. I thought, *Why? I can review it at home, then she can read my reply in ten minutes. It won't cost as much.*

About a month after the holidays, I got an email from her telling me she couldn't represent me anymore. There were "too many incompatibilities."

I was terrified. I had a court order I needed to respond to in a couple of days.

I called a few more attorneys and was told that they couldn't take on any more clients.

The deadline was closing in. When I mentioned it to one attorney, he offered to draft the paperwork I needed. No charge. I thanked him profusely, then took it to the court clerk and submitted it.

I finally found an attorney who was willing to meet with me. A woman, so I was hoping she would be sympathetic. I sat down in the leather chair opposite her broad, clean desk. She said, "I'm going to shut my eyes. I can't concentrate very well with them open."

I thought, *Seriously?*

As our conversation moved forward, she said, *"*What assets do you have?*"*

Suddenly, I realized that she expected me to be willing to sell everything I had to get through the divorce. I thought, *She wants my house.*

I knew what I was up against. I said with a very definite edge, "Fine. You can have my house."

She replied, "I haven't even told you I'd be your attorney."

I got up and left. I still didn't have an attorney, and I had to appear in court. I went alone. Randy didn't show. I stood next to his attorney. I didn't want to have to do it again.

I talked to Tina one afternoon and she said, "I know someone who might be able to help."

I thought, *I need this so much, but I can't get my hopes up.*

I met with Ed Carmington about two weeks later. I told him what I had been doing with the previous attorney to keep costs down. He said he would help. I signed another contract and wrote another check.

Tina helped in ways I could have never predicted, twice, in a short span of time. But as one issue after another arose with Randy, I began to realize I had to walk away from our friendship. Tina was as much of a friend to Randy as she was to me, and it wasn't working. This time at least I could explain it.

Mr. Carmington told me that the previous attorney never submitted our parenting plan. Then Randy told the court that I was an abusive parent, which meant we needed an investigation by a Guardian Ad Litem.

~ ~ ~

Every time Jade and Amber had to visit Randy, I traveled with them on the ferry. When I lived on the island, I heard reports of ferries sinking. One was in Canada. I "knew" none of the ferries were ever going to sink, but I also knew that if one ever did, my kids were going to have their mother with them. When it was my responsibility, they weren't going to have to deal with it alone, depending on the help of strangers.

Our house was visible from the ferry a few minutes after it left the dock. For months, after I dropped the girls off, I cried. It was so hard to imagine Jade and Amber having to go to that house knowing I was going to be somewhere else. When they came home, they often shared difficult stories, and I would spend hours, as Zola offered one day, "giving them a soft place to land."

In some ways the events I had been experiencing were doing the same for me.

For a while I described them as buoys, as if I found something to carry me above the raging, rock-strewn rapids of life. As though I had finally achieved the second stage in Maslow's hierarchy of needs, and I could finally feel safe.[31]

Instead it felt more like I was moving down a sometimes calm, sometimes turbulent river, acquiring a myriad of bumps and bruises, but occasionally landing in a place where I would watch something incredible bloom. Then the waters would shift imperceptibly, and once again, carry me along.

~ ~ ~

For my first meeting with the Guardian Ad Litem, I took a shoebox filled with photos of the girls, copies of the birthday invitations I had created, pictures of cakes I had decorated, Mother's Day cards, and a few beaded trinkets the girls made for me over the years.

She sat way back in her chair as I shared them, staring back at me with a cold, blank look on her face.

I also told her that Jade and Amber were excelling in the advanced programs. When Jade entered seventh grade, she met a couple of kids who were ahead of her in math. She was eleven, but she was sure she could do what they were doing. I paid for a summer math course so she could catch up. Then she joined the math team, and she started attending competitions in nearby cities. Sometimes the team travelled in a school vehicle to places like Mukilteo and Federal Way.

When Amber and I were at the school for Halloween pumpkin carving, we met a family that had a daughter Amber's age. The girl's grandmother, Carolyn, and I had some time to talk. I felt like I finally found someone who wanted to spend time together. We took the girls to the pool and lots of festivals.

I also began to see that while it's difficult for kids to be smart, it's also difficult to be the parent of smart kids.

~ ~ ~

I was still getting work from a couple of long-term clients and found a few new ones in the area, but small, tourist businesses had a different idea about how much time it took to generate an ad or a logo. People were also constantly asking me if I could donate or volunteer.

One day I received a $1000 check I wasn't expecting. As I was driving back from the post office with it in my hand, I realized that, somehow, I was getting enough to make ends meet.

Randy finally sold the boat. I was surprised at the depth of sadness that came over me. It was a beautiful craft, my connection to some of the places I'd felt most connected, Sucia, Jones, and Clark Islands, that encircled Orcas Island as though they were her offspring.

When the check arrived, it went straight to the attorney.

A couple of months later I got a call from the realtor who sold us the house. She asked if I would be interested in a part-time job.

Within a few days, I was raising children, maintaining a home, going through a divorce, and juggling two jobs.

### ~ A R T I F I C E ~

Anacortes thrived by offering festivals, music by the waterfront, bicycle and walking trails, local fishing, and access to the San Juan Islands. I loved the fact that we could easily drive to Mount Vernon, Bellingham, and Seattle.

One afternoon, I drifted over to the bulletin board at the newly remodeled Anacortes Library and noticed a post for a workshop at an alternative church. I did, and I didn't want to go. I was still afraid of people who had different beliefs about God.

But now I was one of them.

~ ~ ~

I stood in front of the door of a building in the commercial part of Old Town. A bright yellow flag waved in the breeze that had the salty tang of the waterfront a couple of blocks away. I opened the door and walked up a narrow stairway wondering about my decision. When I got to the top there was a room to the left and a group of people sitting around a table. I said hello to them, four women and one man, and pulled out a chair that was close to the entry. A woman who was standing on the far side talked to another woman for a few minutes, then she started the workshop.

They were making vision boards.

The facilitator handed out stacks of magazines and told us hand them around and around the group until she said stop. Then she told us to thumb through the one we had until we found an image or word that resonated with our goals or dreams for the year. When everyone was done, we did it again. We shuffled through the magazines five or six times. Then we glued down the pictures and words.

I looked at what I had created and tried to be happy with it. But like most of my creative efforts, I felt like I could have done a better job.

I put it on my fridge when I got home and tried to feel like it had meaning for me, but it felt more like I was trying to shoehorn meaning into it.

Still, everyone seemed nice enough, so I decided to attend one of the services the following Sunday.

When I got there, I could hear voices coming from a room on the far side of the one I had been in the week before. I stood in the entryway to get a bulletin and introduced myself to the pastor. Her name was Bernice. I couldn't help but think there might be potential for a similar kind of a connection with my great aunt, but at that point I felt like I was strong enough to maintain my bearings if it didn't.

The room was big enough to seat about 100 people, and there were about 20 people scattered around. A musician was tuning a guitar on the far side.

After the service some of the members gathered for coffee, tea, and a snack in the room where we made the vision boards. There was also a small kitchen that had been obscured. When I got an opportunity to talk to the pastor, I told her about my aunt, hoping that maybe this time, I had found a home. I was also introduced to the pastor's husband, Roy, the man I had seen at the workshop.

I didn't go every week. I felt like I needed to be sure that it was going to be a good relationship. After a couple of weeks, I struggled with the fact that the pastor was making a repetitive confirmational statement and expecting people to repeat it. I couldn't. I couldn't say I believed it with absolute certainty.

One morning I was sitting in one of the chairs near the door, and Roy was sitting slightly to one side and a couple of rows ahead of me.

People were milling around waiting for the service to start. Pastor Bernice was standing on the platform behind the podium, and I heard Roy say, "It's all a bunch of crap." I sat there trying to figure out what was going on. I didn't know if he had mental health issues or if that's what he believed. He hardly said anything during the services or the gatherings.

The church had a library, so I looked over the books during awkward moments when I was alone or someone excused themselves to get a snack or more coffee. I saw books like *Set Your Heart Free* by Francis de Sales and *The Seven Healing Chakras Workbook* by M.D. Brenda Davies.

The events I had been experiencing did and didn't revolve around my heart, but that wasn't the part I wanted to learn more about. I wasn't looking for healing.

I couldn't speak their language.

# ~ S I G H ~

I was still working on my writing about women's issues and wanted to reread a passage in the *Bible*. I couldn't find my copy, so I picked up another one at a used bookstore. When I finally found the passage again, I couldn't believe what I was seeing.

One word had changed.

In Numbers 5.23 – 5.28, which was about making a woman "drink a water of bitterness that brings the curse," what I remembered as being, uterus, had now become, thigh. "Her womb shall swell and her thigh shall fall away, and the woman shall become a curse among her people." It was a 2005 edition.[32]

A short time later, I found my 1989 version. After I confirmed that I had seen "uterus" in "Numbers" there, I scanned "Matthew" and "Mark" again. I was going to work through the rest of the *New Testament* even if it felt like I was burying myself in a hole and allowing a handful of men to throw rocks at my head.

~ ~ ~

Ah, yes. That's where I left off. The prince of peace:

- Jesus tells his disciples that slaves should be cut up into pieces if they mistreat one another while the "master" is gone.[33]
- Jesus says, "I came to bring fire to the Earth, and how I wish it were already kindled!... Do you think I have come to bring peace to the Earth? No, I tell you, but rather division."[34]
- " I tell you, to all those who have, more will be given; but from those who have nothing, even what they have will be taken away. But for these enemies of mine who did not want me to be king over them—bring them here and slaughter them in my presence."[35]

I thought, *Why would Jesus be any different than the men in the* Old Testament *when that's what he grew up reading about the nature of men and God?*

~ ~ ~

As a child I was mesmerized when I heard the introduction to "John." Now it seemed like a cheap trick, a way to throw people off balance, to make us think it meant more than anything we'd ever heard. Now I couldn't even make it make sense.

In comparison to "Matthew, "Mark," and "Luke," "John's" language had a completely different energy. Where "Matthew" was using flint, "John" was using a flame-thrower. While "Mark" was walking door-to-door selling palm leaf brooms, "John" was trying to sell you your own home.

- John the Baptist says God told him when Spirit descends on someone and stays there, which we are to understand happened with Jesus, that "he baptizes with the Holy Spirit," so John immediately starts telling people, "Here is the Lamb of God who takes away the sins of the world."[36]
- Everyone else immediately says similar things. "We have found the Messiah…We have found him about whom Moses in the law and the prophets wrote, Jesus, son of Joseph from Nazareth. You are the Son of God! You are the King of Israel!"[37]

Jesus has become a completely different person. In the other reports, Jesus says, "Tell no one." He speaks in parables so only a few can understand. In "John," he tells a Samaritan woman (when even speaking to a woman was unusual) that he is the Messiah.[38] At a festival, he says, "I am the light of the world."[39]

~ ~ ~

Jesus continues with another metaphor, telling a group of people in a synagogue that he is the bread of life. He repeats it until the metaphor drops, and he says "…whoever eats me will live because of me."[40] I couldn't help but think about the family in Maccabees.

A short time later Jesus contradicts himself by saying, "It is the spirit that gives life; the flesh is useless."[41]

In John 7, everyone is going to the Festival of Booths. Jesus says he doesn't want to go because the Jews want to kill him. Then "after his brothers had gone, (Jesus) also went, but not publicly, but as it were in secret."[42]

Does anyone care if Jesus lies? It's been in the *Bible* for two thousand years.

Then "John" contradicts what he said about the Spirit in "John 1.32," that he had seen the spirit descending from heaven like a dove . "Now (Jesus) said this about the Spirit, which believers in him were to receive, *for as yet there was no Spirit*, because Jesus was not yet glorified."[43]

~ ~ ~

In "John," Jesus speaks with brazen confidence:

- "I came from God, and now I am here…."[44]
- "Whoever is from God hears the words of God. The reason you do not hear them is because you are not from God. Very truly I tell you, before Abraham was, I am."[45]
- "All who came before me are thieves and bandits. The father and I are one. I am the resurrection and the life."[46]

Frequent, oddly placed reinforcements prop up Jesus.

- "…during supper, Jesus, knowing that the father had given all things to his hands, and that he had come from God and was going to God, got up from the table…."[47]

- When Judas leaves the table, Jesus goes into repetition overdrive: "Now the Son of man has been glorified, and God has been glorified in him. God will also glorify him in himself and will glorify him at once."[48]

Jesus says that he, too, has commandments. "Love one another as I have loved you," but I noticed as I read the next two lines, that he only meant it for their "friends." He says, "No one has greater love than this, to lay down one's life for one's friends. You are my friends if you do what I command you."[49]

Which isn't love. It seems like the sentiments "Do unto others…," and "Love one another…" were only for the select few that followed Jewish law.

Then Jesus makes another statement that clearly indicates he isn't an all-knowing God, "I have conquered the world."[50] It wasn't true then, and it isn't true now.

~ ~ ~

I found one more surprise at the end of "John."

Things.

"John's" last words are, "But there are also many other things that Jesus did…." As if everything he shared wasn't enough. He continues, "…if every one of them were written down, I suppose that the world itself could not contain the books that would be written."[51]

All I could think about was amps.

## ~ R . A . K . ~

The divorce was finalized in the early spring. Four years after the girls and I left the island. Three years of attorney fees.

But Jade and Amber were building robots. Amber had been invited to join an after-school team, and a short time later, Jade found a class called Principles of Technology.

On one of our trips to Orcas, Jade and Amber talked about building the Lego robots. It was hard for me to imagine how you could get something made from Legos to move.

The ferry pulled into the terminal. I walked the girls up the loading dock and waited until I saw them connect with their father, then I turned around, and reboarded. I went up to the passenger deck and sat in one of the seats on the side toward the island. As the ferry backed out, I could see the house that wasn't mine anymore. I watched until it disappeared behind a hill, knowing the girls didn't want to be there.

A wave of despair hit me. I couldn't stop the tears. I made my way down the stairs to my truck and tried to settle down. I didn't have any tissue, so I dabbed my eyes with my sleeve and headed back up to the restroom.

I grabbed some toilet paper, put soap and water on it, and walked over to the mirror in the sitting area away from the faucets, so no one would see me. Something was sitting at the far end of the long shelf that ran underneath. I walked over to see what it was. Someone left a tiny bouquet of flowers, that had completely wilted, on top of a slip of paper.

"You've got a friend! take this home! enjoy, R.A.K."

It felt like the message was for me.

Of course it wasn't. Someone forgot it. I figured they'd come back to get it before they got off the ferry. Then it occurred to me that they might have gotten off at Orcas.

I sat on one of the benches at the back end of the ferry. No one else was sitting in the area. I was able to see the restroom door, and no one entered during the rest of the trip. I knew the note had been left there mistakenly, but I kept wondering if the mistake happened because I was also supposed to get the message. Still, I struggled with the idea of taking something that didn't belong to me.

From the sheer number of times I'd walked on as a passenger instead of driving, I knew walk-ons had to wait on the passenger level for a crew member to open the front gate, so I often saw the crew cleaning up the ferry after each round trip. If no one came for it, I was sure they would toss it into the garbage.

I heard the arrival announcement. No one came down the aisle toward me. Everyone turned into the stairwell to go to their cars or headed toward the front. I went into the restroom and picked it up.

When I got home, I set the piece of paper up against my bathroom mirror. As I looked at it, I didn't break the "signature" into initials, I read it as one word – RAK, rock.

~ ~ ~

I helped Amber during the robot build season, watching the kids, coaching them a little, trying to make sure everyone got a chance to work on the design. Since the group was a new team, they didn't make it far in the playoffs, but the leader decided to hold an end-of-season ceremony. Amber was called to the front along with one of the boys.

The coach stood between them and said, "Amber has been such a great helper, and well, Jeffrey, he got so much done for the team. I call him Mr. Busy Hands."

I stood next to Amber wanting to say something. Knowing I couldn't. But at that point, I decided that if she was going to continue to be on a team, I was going to volunteer as often as I could.

~ ~ ~

Amber was browsing the kid's section of the library. On one of the end caps, I noticed *The Young Person's Guide to Philosophy*. For most of my life philosophy had been like physics – nothing more than words that seemed to circle the planet with an irritating regularity, far beyond my reach.

I picked it up and one of the first questions in the Table of Contents was, "Is there a God?"

I thought, *Really? I thought those discussions only occurred in the realms of religion.*

The author, Jeremy Weate, says that philosophers don't even agree on what Philosophy is, but he said they think about lots of things, and they develop tools to help others learn to think. Weate also said that philosophy and science used to be more closely connected so it made sense that many philosophers had backgrounds in science. When you start to grasp the complexity of the universe, it leads to lots of questions, like, What holds the world together? What part of us survives as we grow older? Are we products of nature or nurture?

One afternoon I closed the book and looked at the cover, where one of the most famous philosophical quotes, "I think, therefore I am" was featured. I couldn't help but think, *Rocks and little bouquets of flowers don't think, but they certainly are something.*

## ~ R O O K I E S ~

I finally finished what I thought was a final draft of my book about my experiences as a woman and a mother. I contacted a quick printer on San Juan Island and asked if they could produce a couple of copies, spiral bound. Then I asked Zola if she would read it. I waited patiently, and a couple of weeks later, she gently reminded me that what I had written was too personal.

Understanding hit me immediately. Like she just had to open the edge of the package, and I knew it was foul. I'd been reading essays in women's magazines. No one was including the same kind of details. It was incredibly discouraging, but I told myself, I had content I could work from, I was learning about craft, and somehow I could figure it out.

I still wanted to speak from experience and thought, *If I can't speak directly about my life because of concerns about libel, I'll have to abstract my thoughts about marriage, sexuality, relationships, and religion. I'll try humor.*

Apparently I needed a heavy dose of comic relief. My mind went into hyperdrive as I worked on essays like "One Smokin' Hot Babe," "Adam and Eve Get It On," and "Relationship Roulette" while dreaming about connecting with like-minded writers.

~ ~ ~

The parents and students in Jade's Principle of Technology course were introduced to the program, *FIRST* Robotics, at the high school one evening. We were told about the costs and asked if we were interested in forming a team. Every parent raised their hand in support. The students were going to be building 120-pound robots, following strict guidelines, over a period of six weeks, then take them to events—local, regional, and national—to compete in alliances.

The students met after school a couple of days later to select a team leader. A few of them decided that it would be best to have three, and Jade was chosen as one of them.

There were lots of preparations to do before Kickoff in early January. Jade worked in an administrative capacity and applied her artistic talents to multiple projects. Then, when they started working on the robot, she designed the robot's articulating arm. At a local competition, the Regional Director of

*FIRST* noticed her efforts.

Then the team made it to regionals, which was held in downtown Seattle at Key Center.

Carolyn and her granddaughter, Serena, joined Amber and I to watch the competition. It was hard to see much of anything, but Carolyn and Serena were patient as we waited for the rounds when Jade's team competed as part of an alliance. The team didn't place high enough to be in the final round, so Serena asked if we could go out to the fountain.

I watched with trepidation as she went halfway down into the basin of the fountain and got sprinkled while Amber tiptoed around the upper edge. Then Serena went all in. I watched her for a few minutes and thought, *She has to be getting cold. We should probably get going.*

There was a lot of noise in the area, but I suddenly realized that one of the sounds was my phone ringing. When I answered it was really hard to figure out what the person was saying. Then I heard Jade screaming, "Where are you?"

I said, "Serena wanted to come out to the fountain." Then I raised the volume, "We're still at the Center. At the fountain!"

"You're still here?"

"Yes."

"Come back in! We won Rookie of the Year! They're going to be making the presentation in a few minutes!"

I couldn't believe what her team had accomplished.

I couldn't believe we were still there. If Carolyn and Serena hadn't been with us, if they hadn't asked about going out to the fountain, we would have been 20 minutes up the freeway.

I didn't miss the moment.

I wanted to kiss the universe.

# TREES

I STILL RECEIVED MONTHLY PRINT ISSUES of *Columns*, the University of Washington alumni magazine. They usually sat on my living room table collecting dust for a couple of months, then I'd move them into the garbage, annoyed, but reminding myself I could only do so much.

The March 2009 Edition, the same month the divorced had been finalized, had been sitting on the table, and I picked it up. The inquiry on the cover intrigued me: "Why Do We Need Art? Ellen Dissanayake (pronounced diss-an-eye-akuh) May Have the Answer."

She believed that we create art to make things special. The essay resonated with me, but it wasn't going to change my life.

I turned the page and read the next article, "Tribal Counsel: The voices of Native Americans are being heard as never before at the UW" by Julie Garner.

In this essay, the "special" nature of art seemed to leap into another dimension.

When a member of the Chillawack Tribe, Herb Joe, was born in 1945, he was given the ancestral name, T'xwelátse. He was told it was his duty to bring T'xwelátse, a long-lost, four-foot granite statue of the tribe's first male ancestor, back to the Chillawack Tribe.

In 2006, he did.

We create art to make things special.

Like making a four-foot granite statue. Could the artist have known how special the statue would be? They couldn't have known, could they, that over time it would connect to this young man, his namesake? I didn't believe that the art I created in college had any special properties, but within my lifetime, that changed.

This exceedingly special event had a level of complexity that was similar to the events I'd been experiencing. The first powerful event that I recognized connected to the most important ancestor in my life, Aunt Bernice. The way the focus of the article by Dissanayake tied into it added another dimension.

~ ~ ~

As a child, if I heard the word, ancestor, it didn't register. As a young woman, I was told that we found true power by having courage, developing self-esteem, and working hard.

## ~ M I N D S P A C E . 4 2 ~

But "ancestors" was the first "power" word I listed when I started to take notes from books I was reading that included *Reviving Ophelia* by Mary Pipher PhD and Sara Gilliam; *Without a Net: The Female Experience of Growing Up Working Class* by Michelle Tea; *The Bitch In the House* by Cathi Hanauer; and *Born to Rebel* by Frank J. Sulloway.

Bunny McCune tells us in *Girls to Women: Women to Girls*, that if she had known "about prehistory when she was thirteen, she would have had more of a chance to resist all the forces that were trying to change her true self. Artifacts tell us their makers were peaceful people who saw the female as divine."[52]

~ ~ ~

Amber often picked up the movies *Mulan* and *Spirited Away*. I was glad she was watching movies with strong female leads, so I joined her a couple of times, but the part about Mulan's ancestors was difficult for me. I didn't believe that spirits of the dead had any kind of power.

I was surprised at how often Amber watched *Spirited Away*. On one of our adventures to Alderwood Mall, we stopped in Borders bookstore. I could have gotten lost on the first level, but we eventually made our way up to the second. A few minutes later, I heard Amber yell, "They have *Spirited Away!*" The figure, No Face, was going to be living with me, every day. At one point I talked to Amber about it, and she told me that she liked the fact that none of the characters were wholly bad or wholly good. I remembered reading something similar, so I brought up the document with my book notes.

The first book I chose to take notes from, Dhyani Ywahoo's book, *Voices of Our Ancestors: Cherokee Teachings from the Wisdom Fire*, said:

"Even the worst person has the seed of good within, and even the most positive person can make errors from seed of ignorance. Negative action can be the seed of realizing the good."[53]

Amber was able to see this in a movie as a small child. I had to live it and hope that somehow people would recognize that I had learned from my mistakes.

It wasn't until I was in my mid-30s that I found out through my father's research that we had ancestors of note. A civil war hero. Family names on the Ellis Island wall. I shared them with the girls and dreamed of being able to stand in the same places.

## ~ THE SANCTUARY ~

I attended a book reading at the library one evening. While I was waiting to get my book signed, I struck up a conversation with the woman in front of me.

"What kind of work do you do?" she asked.

Even though it seemed like we had reached that point rather quickly, I didn't hesitate to answer.

"Graphic design. But it's tough around here."

"It's kind of crazy, but I have some information that might help. I saw a job post for a graphic designer. You should check it out."

I thanked her and searched for it the next day.

Two days later, I was being interviewed. We took a tour of the building and things seemed to be a little quiet, but I didn't know what the work schedules were, so I didn't give it any more thought.

I was offered the job and gave notice to my manager at the real estate office. The kind of work I was doing in the new position was in my field and paid reasonably well.

I thought, *I've finally made it! We can stop worrying about money.*

I couldn't help but think about the way it came to be. A conversation with a random person at the library.

~ ~ ~

Within a few weeks, I began to wonder about the decision. I moved forward with hardware and software setup, but I was getting mixed responses about my progress from my manager. I coordinated with publications about the launch of a new product. I produced ads and sent out email announcements, but something didn't feel right.

I had already started to deep-clean my house and yard early in the Spring when the real estate office started cutting my hours, so as summer approached, I continued. In some ways I wanted to be free of the house. It was so hard to take care of it alone. The location created one problem after another during the winter months, and I couldn't keep up with repairs.

I swept out the wood shed, the breeding ground of sumo-wrestler-sized spiders. I vacuumed the ceiling and walls in the garage that had gaps around the doors that allowed the spiders to find their forever home and enough hidey holes to keep me from locating all of the them. I used a steel brush to clean the moss off of the railroad ties that surrounded the driveway and formed the entrance to the front stairway. I threw away the beloved paper remnants I still had from projects I did in college.

In the middle of July, five months later, my manager and a woman from Human Resources came into my office with a letter informing me that I was being laid off.

I didn't have enough work to pay the bills.

~ ~ ~

I talked to Amber and Jade about our options. I longed to move to Seattle, and Jade knew it.

"This is your chance," she said. "You can make the move now. You have family in the Seattle area. I'll be leaving for college next year, anyway."

Suddenly, I was hit with a reality that made me sick. I was going to lose the house, and I couldn't take the birds with me.

I cried for days, trying to think of a way I could make it work. I talked to everyone I could think of. My mother even offered a suggestion: try to find a sanctuary.

There was a guy who brought his macaws to Anacortes during festivals. I kept the newspaper clipping, so I looked up his number. He told me he could take them, but that his birds lived outside, and he didn't think mine would make it through the winter.

I talked to veterinarians to see if they might be willing to keep them for a few months until I could find a job and get a new place, then I realized I couldn't keep them in an apartment. I found a sanctuary north of Seattle. The owner told me she would take them, but said once she did, I couldn't see them again. She mentioned a place in south Seattle, and the owner said he would take them.

~ ~ ~

Jade was in her senior year of high school, and still a leader on the robotics team so she didn't want to leave. She talked to a couple of friends, and a family offered her a place to stay.

I called the realtor who sold me the house and put it back on the market. I bought bathroom towels, that none of us would use. I painted the front porch, that Amber had somersaulted down one afternoon (without so much as a bruise). I put flowers in containers by the entrance.

My parents offered their spare room.

Amber was still visiting her father a few weekends a year, so I planned to come back to the house every couple of weeks to take care of maintenance. Most of my mail went to a post office box, so there would only be junk in the mailbox.

I didn't think it would take more than a couple of months to find work. I didn't have the truck anymore, but there was a large space in the back of my car.

The move took a couple of trips because I needed to bring a desk and my computer equipment. We stopped at the school and Amber registered for sixth grade. I was happy to see it was a reasonable walking distance from my parents' apartment. On one of the trips, the school called to tell me Amber needed to take a placement test to determine her math level, so we set up another appointment.

~ ~ ~

I turned onto the gravel lane that led to the sanctuary. A gorgeous log house was positioned at the end. To the right, a well-manicured lawn that looked like a city park disappeared into 60-foot evergreens surrounding the property. A narrow dirt road ran down a hill to the left that appeared to terminate in front of a traditional red barn.

The owner approached and gave me a tour. We walked the inside perimeter of acres of evergreens that extended past his house to the north, then we walked to the south end of the property, where ten to fifteen cages were positioned in clearings.

"They're heavy-duty, portable garages," he said. "We've taken in hundreds of birds that needed homes for one reason or another. Sometimes a person passes on and no one in the family can take it. Sometimes the birds are too aggressive."

It was August so it was warm. "What do you do in the winter?" I asked.

"We cover them. It blocks the wind. Then we shovel bark into the bottom of the cages. As it composts it gives off heat. We have an arrangement with a logging company. They bring us truckloads. There's some over there."

I thought, *That can't be enough when it drops below freezing,* as I was looking at hundreds of birds enjoying the sunshine.

When I got Kiroc, I thought she would be with me forever. I didn't know until after we got her that Macaws could live to be in their eighties. By that time, I figured I could find someone to take her. I had no idea how intelligent macaws were until we got Rocket. He never said his own name, but he said, "Kiroc." Kiroc did the same. She would hear me chastising Rocket, telling him to get back up on his perch, and she would help, "Rocket, get up there. Get back up there." When I first got Kiroc, she would repeat, "Where's a kiss?" Shortly after Rocket arrived, she stopped.

I tried to find a way to accept the situation. I thought, *They've had physical comfort but no community. Now they'll have much more difficult lives, but they*

154

*will have a chance to be part of a community.*

For the next couple of weeks as I made one arrangement after another for the move, I cried. I stood in the doorway of the room to their cages and cried. I cried when I sat with them outside. I talked to them constantly about what was going to happen. I told them how much I was going to miss them.

Then the day came that we had to go. Amber came with me. She helped position the travel carrier so they could see the journey as we drove down the freeway. Then as we headed into back country. Up and over hills. Down roads that followed winding creeks lined with a lime-colored canopy.

We parked the car in front of the log house. Some of the Macaws were screaming about the disturbance. I took Rocket out first. His wings went out, flapping, as I held on to his claws. He was ready to join them. But he couldn't. They had to go into isolation for a couple of weeks to make sure they didn't have any kind of disease.

I told Kiroc and Rocket we would be back. It was something I said to them every time I left for as long as I had them. All I could do was hope they understood. The owner said I could visit as often as I wanted. But I was hardly able to hold myself together as I forced the words out to say that we'd be back in a couple of weeks.

~ F L O O R E D ~

Jade was on a winning robotics team. She was a talented artist, highly skilled in math, and she also was a soprano in the high school choir. She sang a solo at a school concert, and her team traveled to Bellingham for a competition where they won an award.

Jade also won recognition for her efforts on the robotics team from the local chapter of the American Association of University Women, and I joined her for the event. As part of her award, she was offered a choice from a collection of books. She told me she had plenty to read with her school work, so she said, "Why don't you pick what you want?" Still, since it was for her, I chose one that seemed like it would have the most value later in her life, *Nobel Prize Women in Science, Second Edition,* by Sharon Bertsch McGrayne. Of course, I promptly began to read it.

As Jade accumulated awards and recognition, I kept wondering how it was making Amber feel. She had created some amazing artwork, and she received recognition on one of her essays from the elementary school principal, so I tried to make sure she knew that she was just as capable. But I felt like I did when Jade was in kindergarten. I didn't really know what that meant.

When the new school called about the results from the math test, they answered my question. They said that Amber would be placed at the 8th grade level. I thought, *How are these girls doing this?*

~ ~ ~

I did my best to support Amber as she transitioned to the new school. Then I started to look for work. I wanted to get a job in my field. One that would pay well and offer benefits. I knew what was expected. I was supposed to be able to create motion graphics, so I tried to learn how to use Adobe Flash.

My parents set up an air mattress on the floor for Amber, which left about a foot of space between it and the futon where I would be sleeping. The first time Amber moved on the mattress, it squeaked. I thought, *OMG. I'm not going to be able to sleep.* There was a large window at the far end of the room where I had positioned my desk and a small window high up on the side wall, which we figured we could leave open at night since it was still August, but even though we were on the third floor, and it had to be over 80 degrees in that space, my parents wouldn't let us.

Amber came home after the third or fourth day at school and told me that they were teaching the material she covered last year.

"No problem," I said. "I'll talk to the principal and get documentation transferred from the Challenge program."

I made an appointment with the principal and explained everything.

"We can't do that," he said. "Our decisions about moving students ahead are made in the spring. It's school policy."

I said, "She tested into eighth-grade math. I can connect you with her teacher."

He replied, "There isn't any way we can do it. I'm sorry. There's always the option of homeschooling."

~ ~ ~

*Sure*, I thought as I drove home. *I can look for a job, drive 100 miles every other weekend to maintain a home, and manage homeschooling on top of it.* As I continued to process the impact it was going to have on us, I thought, *What happens when I get a job and we move into another apartment? Amber will be left home alone. For ten-plus hours a day.*

I acted like I was going to be able to figure out something when I talked to Amber. A couple of days passed and at about 11:00 p.m. she told me she wasn't feeling well.

"Don't worry," I said. "I'll call and excuse you in the morning."

It was a miserable night. I got up when she was supposed to be getting ready for school and let my parents know.

I went back into the room and tried to rest. About fifteen minutes later, the washing machine started. It was right outside our door.

I got back up and asked my mother if it could wait an hour, if we could keep it quiet a little longer to let Amber get some more rest.

My father was in the kitchen, and he blew up.

"You are a guest here. We're old. It's not our job to accommodate you.

We have our schedules. It's hard enough for us to have to try to deal with all of this."

I sat down at the dining room table. My mother was sitting on the opposite side. I looked at her hoping she would say it was okay, that she could wait. But she wouldn't. I waited a few more seconds hoping she would speak up, for once. She just sat there, staring back at me in silence.

I got up and went back to the bedroom and stayed there as much as I could throughout the day. There had been other problems. Other comments that didn't make any sense. Other rules that were making our lives miserable.

I thought, *Why did I think this was going to work?*

I spent the rest of the day trying to figure out how to make it work, but when I woke up the next morning, I knew we had to leave. I called the family Jade was staying with to see if they might be able to help. All they could do was offer a suggestion. It was good enough. We'd rent a truck.

~ ~ ~

It was Friday. Amber and I left mid-afternoon as we had been doing many weekends. As we were driving, I talked to Jade about what was happening. I felt like I was going to have a nervous breakdown. I was moving back to a house that I was sure was going to foreclose out from under me, and I had forgotten about the fact that Amber was no longer in the Challenge program.

It was after 3:00 pm. I asked Amber to call directory assistance to get the number for the school in Anacortes.

When the receptionist picked up, I asked her if the principal was in. When she said yes, I told her our situation was urgent and she put me on hold. She came back on the line and told me the principal was available.

I explained our situation as quickly as I could.

"We understand that these kinds of things can happen," he said. "We hold a couple of spaces open for them."

I couldn't believe what I was hearing. At that moment it was the only thing that mattered. I thanked the principal profusely and let him know she would be there Monday.

~ ~ ~

We had to wait until 4:30 p.m. Saturday to get the truck. We picked up Jade right afterwards so we could leave Sunday morning at 7 a.m. When we got to my parent's house, we loaded all of our belongings into the bed of the truck and cleaned the room as best we could.

We were back in Anacortes mid-afternoon. I planned to make the best use I could of the truck. Every dollar mattered at that point. We dumped Amber's and my things in the living room, the entry, and the garage, then we headed to the place Jade was staying to move as much as we could. We got done around dinner time, and went back to the house to unload again.

I took the kids to school Monday morning, then I took the truck back. I got my computer set up, checked to see what work I needed to do, then I started putting things away. The house was on the market. I could get a call any day. I wasn't expecting it. There hadn't been any calls up until that point, but I didn't want to take any chances.

My phone rang on Wednesday.

"I have a client that wants to look at your house. Would tomorrow be okay?"

"Sure. What time?"

"Does 11:00 a.m. work?"

"Sure."

"Thank you. No one should be in the home at the time."

"Yes, of course. Thank you."

There was a mess in the kitchen sink. There was a mess in the living room.

I cleaned and hid things. I vacuumed and figured I'd do it again just before I left. On my way out the door the next morning, I grabbed one of my threadbare towels and wiped down the front steps.

~ ~ ~

My realtor called the next day. "We've got an offer," she said.

"Oh, my God. That's wonderful."

"I'm not sure it will work. Why don't you come by and we'll go over it."

I went to the office a couple hours later. The couple wanted the house for about $10,000 less than then what I owed.

I said, "Unfortunately I can't pay them to take it." I felt like I was losing the only buyer that would show before I burned through my savings.

~ ~ ~

A couple of days later, I got another call from the same Realtor asking if the couple could see the house again.

I cleaned, polished, and vacuumed. I wiped down the front steps as I left, then I waited in the adjoining cul-de-sac.

That afternoon I had an offer I could live with.

I was stunned. I had a buyer. I didn't know where I was going to get more work, but I had a buyer.

The proceeds gave me enough money to feel like I could make it through the school year. To get Jade through graduation and figure out what I needed to do from there.

I found an apartment in the middle of town that worked for us. I packed for the move while I managed the projects I had in the works. Just before the end of the month, the phone rang.

"This is Kent Bosworth," a deep voice said. "I introduced myself to you at the real estate office. I have a couple of projects I need help with. I picked up a guidebook, and I'll need a couple of websites. Would you be willing to work with a web developer?"

"Yes, I would," I said as calmly as I could manage. "I've been looking for an opportunity like this for five years. When would you like to meet?"


## ~ U N O B S T R U C T E D   V I S I O N ~


I finally understood why my mother had to be Hestia.

Fitting the "old-fashioned idea of 'a good wife.' Quiet, unassertive, anonymous." She seemed to be able to muster up some affection for my father, but with me, she was, "detached, impersonal, undemonstrative."[54]

When Maya suggested I read Jean Shinoda Bolen's *Goddesses in Everywoman*, I felt like I had a better understanding of her. But it wasn't until we left my parent's house that Friday morning that I could see Hestia clearly.

It supported my belief that all of this was destined. We had to go back to Anacortes. She had to sit there and allow it to happen, to not interfere.

I was finally able to accept the fact that she would never be there for me, but it was who she had to be, in what seemed to be a way to propel Amber forward, to get her to the place she needed to be.

Amber's sixth grade teacher gave her the opportunity to self-study Algebra.

After that, like Jade, Amber was allowed to skip a grade.


~ ~ ~


My head was spinning given everything that had happened, including the fact that the sale of the house and the new business client allowed all of us to be together for Jade's senior year. A couple of weeks later, Jade told me she had applied to a number of colleges, which included Harvard, Yale, and MIT.

"Why are you applying to Harvard and MIT? I can't afford that."

"When I was making a presentation at a fundraiser a couple of weeks ago, one of the Kiwanis members told me that the tuition is need-based."

"What is need-based?"

"They review your income and figure out what you can afford. That's all you have to pay."

"That would be incredible, but still, MIT? It's just engineers. What about your art?"

"If I get into MIT, who cares? I can do artwork any time."

She told me she had gotten a letter of recommendation from the school superintendent. It was impressive.

"They don't want students that only do math," Jade said as our conversation continued. "They want kids that are creative. People who can create *and* build."

I knew the odds. I figured maybe she'd get accepted at one of the other colleges, but MIT was the best engineering school in the world.

Just before Christmas break, Jade told me that MIT was going to be calling students to let them know if they had been accepted. She invited a friend over to stay the night while she waited to see if she was going to get the call.

I listened to the girls talking in her room. Quiet murmurs and a giggle now and then. At about 9:30 p.m. the phone rang. I couldn't hear what Jade was saying, but by the time I got to the room, she was jumping around, screaming, "I made it! I'm going to MIT! Oh, my God!"

I got to be there for it. I got to be with her at that moment. I wasn't a hundred miles away.

# CHAPTER THREE | THE BEAST

MY COLLECTION OF ESSAYS WAS READY.

Work had become incredibly demanding, but I finally had the means to attend a writer's conference to see if I would be lucky enough to find an agent. Was I holding one of the golden tickets? Would I be escorted into the inner sanctum of the publishing industry?

~ ~ ~

I brought a three-page synopsis.

When I got to the hotel Friday morning, I saw a line of people that snaked around a corner. I stepped into the queue and listened. Writers were signing up for one of four programs of lectures and pitch sessions. Each one included different topics and different agents. The line forked near the end, and the best choice for me was the first pitch session. It seemed crazy, but I thought, *Why not get it over with?* I walked back down the hall and saw a room with a bunch of tables where people appeared to be waiting for the presentations to begin, so I sat down.

A sheet of paper sitting in the middle of the table offered information about the agent pitch sessions.

It explained that there would be lines of chairs in front of each agent, so we had to be strategic, to either get in a long line for our top priority or wait for that line to get shorter by pitching alternative agents. After we finished each pitch, we had to go to the back of the next line. They said to expect three or four opportunities. Then I saw something that confused me. It said the pitches would only be five minutes.

My pitch was three pages. I was sure I read that on the website. I asked people around me, and they said we would actually only get about three minutes because the agent would need a couple of minutes to respond to us.

I had chosen the first session. The next day. 1:00 p.m.

~ ~ ~

I couldn't attend my afternoon lectures. I still wasn't done with my revisions by the time they served dinner. It was close to midnight when I decided I could live with it.

I got up at 6:00 a.m. It felt like old times, catching the red-eye. I attended my selection of morning lectures, then after lunch, I waited in a hall with the other writers who were also scheduled to pitch their books. When they opened the doors, it was like watching the gates open at a rock concert. People ahead of me surged forward, grabbing the front seats as I tried to get oriented.

Still, I felt like I made good presentations. I managed to get three business cards.

~ ~ ~

As we exited the room, someone mentioned that writers were pitching agents in the hallways. Another person said it was okay as long as the agent wasn't preoccupied i.e. making a beeline to the restroom.

Later that afternoon, I was standing by an elevator when an agent approached. He had been in my session but I hadn't been able to pitch my work to him. I decided to see if I could pull it off. He was on his phone as we entered the elevator, then as we exited, he hung up. He asked me to follow him into a wide hallway that had central seating cushions. We sat down and talked for a few minutes. It was encouraging. Then he said, "I don't usually do things like this. I'm married."

I thanked him for his time and left.

~ ~ ~

That evening, exhausted, pissed off, alone in my room, but still imagining that I might still have one of those golden tickets, I thought about how people would respond to my book, Randy included.

Some people were writing under pseudonyms. I wondered if that would be a good idea.

~ ~ ~

Sunday morning everyone gathered in a large room to listen to the closing speaker. She told us writers had to have an internet presence. I thought, *Great. More work.*

She asked if anyone in the group wanted to share the title of their work and a two-minute pitch. I figured it couldn't hurt, maybe someone would be interested. I raised my hand.

As I shared the title, I thought, *I wonder if I should be doing this.* Brave New Girls *is a great title. What if someone uses it before I can get my book published?*

I did my best to condense the theme of the essays into a few sentences, and I ended by saying that I'd found a way for everyone to find peace with abortion.

~ ~ ~

It came from the last chapter of the second edition of the *Nobel Prize Women in Science (NPWS)*, the book I'd selected at the award ceremony for Jade in her senior year.

Two years after *NPWS* was published, Christianne Nüsslein-Volhard won the Nobel Prize in Physiology/Medicine. Sharon Bertsch McGrayne said, "Nüsslein-Volhard's Nobel made a new and expanded edition...necessary."[55]

She went on to say, "Nüsslein-Volhard was one of the most important developmental biologists of all time. She helped explain one of life's greatest mysteries: how a single cell becomes a complex creature like a fruit fly, a fish, or a human being."[56]

She also shared one of Nüsslein-Volhard's other discoveries: "that nearly half of all pregnancies end in spontaneous abortion."[57]

~ ~ ~

Women's bodies are designed to abort unwanted pregnancies.

I thought, *This is going to change the world.*

Later I heard some women say that no one needs a reason to have an abortion, but I knew that many women were against it because of their belief in the *Bible*'s sixth commandment, "Thou shall not kill."

But, I reasoned, if someone believed that God created women, and now understood that women's bodies regularly end life through miscarriage, how could they argue that it's any different than abortion?

The crucial issue for many anti-choicers is that "life" starts at conception.

For the people who believe that: Do you know what God does with the "souls" of those who are miscarried? How do you know that God wouldn't do the same for the "souls" of the aborted?

Many people, like me, struggle with the reasoning of people who claim to be pro-life when there are other forms of killing that we, as a society, accept.

Killing in self-defense (which is how I view abortion). Killing in defense of others who are being violently oppressed (often with our military, which many people in both camps support). Killing the lives of insects, fish, birds, animals, etc. with our feet, our cars, our dams, our jets, our food systems, the production of chemicals used in every industrial process (but pro-lifers are rarely the ones on the frontline of the battle for the environment).

~ ~ ~

After the final presentation, I stood up and collected my paperwork .I heard a man's voice saying, "Who was it that was talking about abortion?"

I turned around and the man approached saying, "I would love to know what you found."

I told him my pitches went well, so I hoped I'd have an agent and publisher in the near future. We continued talking as we walked to the room where they were selling the speaker's books. Shortly before we exchanged email addresses, he mentioned he was a doctor.

I told myself, Don't. Even. Think About. It.

But as we went our separate ways, I wondered if I would ever be able to find someone who shared at least a few things in common with me.

## ~ CALLING MY NAME ~

A couple of weeks later, I had one of those kind-of-cute, kind-of-common moments. As I walked past a group of people gathered at a fund-raising event to support the sanctuary where my parrots now lived, I saw a woman wearing the same shirt I had on.

Of course, women are told that this is their worst nightmare, that somehow it's humiliating, but this wasn't a high-fashion event, so I walked up and said,

"It looks like we should know each other or something!"

The woman laughed and told me her daughter gave it to her. We both turned from side to side, showing off the pink and green floral patterns that surrounded a silver riveted African Gray.

We shared a few more inconsequential comments, but I didn't mention that it actually was an extravagant purchase for me. When I found it along the back wall of a department store, it wasn't something I would normally buy. But when I held it up to show Amber, I decided it would be nice to have something special to wear to the event.

"Yours has longer sleeves," she said.

"Oh, yeah, yours has short ones."

"I prefer three-quarters, but, on a day like today, it's nice to be a little cooler."

There wasn't any reason to hang around, so I told them it was nice to meet them and wandered off to check out the silent auction tables.

~ ~ ~

A short time later, Roy called everyone for the live auction. We gathered together on the large central lawn in somewhat of a scattered circle.

I was surprised to see that a framed print I wanted the year before was up for bid again. I loved the playful green parrots that were surrounded by a matting of deep, earthy green—a color that made me want to buy just about anything—but this year they'd included a signed copy of the book, *The Wild Parrots of Telegraph Hill.*

With the changes in my life, I really didn't need any more artwork, but I'd come to support the event and thought I'd enjoy it, so I bid. Someone else bid up, so I bid again.

The auctioneer was working the crowd talking to the bidders, egging them on to bid higher, so she came my way.

"What's your name?" she asked as she moved the microphone my way.

"Ceejae."

Then she asked me why I wanted it.

I'm not very good at off-the-cuff comments, so I mumbled something about having Macaws, but loving all birds.

The price went above what I wanted to spend, so I dropped out, reminding myself I didn't have that kind of money, and that I had my name on a couple of items in the silent auction, so after the live auction I headed that way.

~ ~ ~

I decided to stay by the table and bid up to whatever it took to make sure I got my choices: a brightly colored, embroidered macaw on a black pillow and a hummingbird figurine. But as the minutes passed, I started to think about the fact that I really didn't need them. I tried to justify sticking around by telling myself that I wanted to contribute and knew I would enjoy them. As I stood there, another woman came up to the table and looked at the bidding sheet.

The decision started to weigh on me. It was miserable standing there alone, watching everyone else with their friends. I wanted to go home. I thought, *I should just let her have it. I can make a cash donation* But I continued to stand there, telling myself I deserved them as much as anyone.

I glanced up and saw a little girl heading my direction.

Her head was tipped down. Her eyebrows practically a straight line. She marched up to me with her arms swinging and a couple of people in tow. She looked straight into my eyes and said, "What's your name?"

I replied, "Ceejae."

She gestured to one of the women behind her, the woman I'd talked to earlier. She said, "My grandmother's name is C.J., too."

~ ~ ~

The woman had the same shirt and the same name, and her granddaughter put it together.

I didn't see them in the circle, but the little girl was apparently paying attention and had seen me because I made a bid. Because the auctioneer was asking everyone to say their names over the loudspeaker.

We talked about how remarkable it was. I asked the woman where she lived.

"Arizona," she said. She was visiting her daughter and granddaughter for the weekend.

I was trying to process what had just happened on top of all of the other events I'd experienced. I wanted to share more, but I felt like I would be crossing some kind of belief-system boundary. That it would be too much, as if no one was allowed to experience anything else. That the proper way to deal with it was to just laugh, smile, and walk away.

~ ~ ~

It felt like I had been called by name. I was in a place, literally draped in it, that couldn't have had any deeper meaning.

CHAPTER THREE | THE BEAST

# HUMANITY

I CREATED A STYLIZED CHARACTER OF MYSELF for my online presence, but somehow lost the sex appeal of the figure I tried to copy.

It was probably a good thing. My initial bios for Facebook and Twitter said, "Hell bent on illuminating a new kind of feminism."

I posted essays like, "Fear of Men," "New Faces of Feminism," and "They," but they were too one-dimensional. Magazines like *Bitch* and *Jezebel* were providing a more than adequate supply of reading material, parsing similar issues through the lens of pop culture, celebrities, and politicians.

I slowly tiptoed over the edge into the life I was living.

~ ~ ~

In the fall, after Amber skipped eight-grade, she joined the high school Robotics team and mentored the middle school Lego League. That year, the robots had to throw frisbees and climb a pole in the last fifteen seconds. The coach divided the students into multiple subsystems: one for the chassis, one for the frisbee-throwing mechanism, one for the lifting mechanism, and one for software and electronics.

Jade tried to talk Amber out of being on the team, but it was all Amber had known. She wanted to be able to apply her skills in the engineering world. She loved woodshop. She made a stepstool with decorative and utilitarian embellishments and a picture frame using tongue and groove joinery. Then she moved on to metal shop.

Bosworth kept me busy with his guidebooks and websites, which we were producing with the open-source software, Drupal. He also found a couple of local clients who wanted sites, and I did, as well. I was able to access the CSS and make a few adjustments, but when I tried to use Drupal on my own, I was back to trying to hack my way through another coding jungle.

Once again, I gave up trying. I had enough to keep myself busy, perfecting everything, volunteering as often as I could to help Amber, reading all I could get my hands on about belief systems, trying to find an online community, and working on my writing.

~ ~ ~

I floated around the internet, joining websites and Facebook groups promoting spirituality. I listened to people talk about angels, pagans, divination, and prophecy like everyone thought they were at the Agora of Athens.

Wait. No. That was in the "Acts of the Apostles."

Spiritual groups focused more on lightworkers, starseeds, astral traveling, crystals, stillness, silence, not taking our thought too seriously, and the Law of Attraction.

Amber and I often walked over to see Carolyn and Serena. They lived down the hill from the house we previously owned. One afternoon Carolyn handed me the book, *A New Earth: Awakening to Your Life's Purpose* by Eckhart Tolle saying, "I don't know if you'd be interested in this. It's not something I want to read." I scanned the cover. I felt like I had already, finally, found my life's purpose. Still, it was by the author of another popular book, *The Power of Now*, so I thought it might at least be worth a quick review. I put it in my Should-I-keep-this-or-throw-it-away? pile.

It was hard for me to be too critical of anything at that point. I went back and forth. When I was pregnant with Amber, I actually wished upon a star one evening to remind the universe that I wanted another girl. Was that the Law of Attraction or probability? I was 99% sure I knew the answer because I also had the personal experience of checking my bank account every month to confirm that I still wasn't a millionaire.

No one in the spiritual groups wanted to talk about being different or being unique. It was all about being one. I was a thistle in a field of flowers. I saw lots of positive posts about Eckart Tolle's work, so I decided to read *A New Earth*.

Page after page contradicted the direction of my thinking, but I couldn't say anything in the spiritual groups. Tolle had a huge following. No one criticized anything anyone was saying or doing. Everyone was positive, helpful, and incredibly sure of themselves.

## ~ THE SNOWPLOW ~

The first year Jade attended MIT, we couldn't afford to get her a flight home for the holidays. But the second year, she got financial help. I hardly went anywhere, so I spaced out car maintenance farther than the recommendations, sometimes six months, sometimes longer.

I needed to pick Jade up at Sea-Tac airport and felt like I needed to get the service done before I drove down. The only appointment available was the morning of Jade's arrival. I wasn't worried, Jade was arriving at 9:00 p.m.

I stayed in the waiting area, reading and glancing at the TV screen every so often. I happened to be looking that way when I saw a weather report. Snow was coming that evening.

I had another split emotional response: I was thankful I had gotten the information so I could figure out how to deal with it and terrified because my car couldn't handle the snow. It wouldn't stop, even when there was just a dusting, which I got to experience one day at the entrance to a roundabout where the slope wasn't much higher than a gopher mound.

I told Amber that Jade and I might have to stay at a hotel, and if the snow was heavy, I couldn't tell her for sure when we'd get home. She made plans to stay with a friend, and I left at about 1:00 p.m. The report said the snow could start any time after 4:00 p.m., so I wanted to make sure I arrived at the airport before rush hour.

Near Southcenter, the roads were dry. I felt like an idiot and went into the mall. Anxiety got the best of me. I couldn't see outside. I headed to the airport terminal and waited just outside the parking garage.

I parked the car at about 7:00 p.m. and found out the flight wouldn't be arriving until about 11:00 pm.

When Jade exited the gate, she looked beat. She said she was sick. I explained the situation with the snow while thinking I needed to get her home. As we crossed the bridge to the parking lot, I looked at the road. It was still clear. We went to the car, and Jade dropped the seat into a reclining position.

I merged onto I-5. After about 15 minutes we were speeding under Freeway Park by the Seattle Convention Center. There still wasn't any sign of snow.

The roads were clear in Lynnwood, 20 miles north, as well as when we passed Highway 2, the highway to Monroe and the macaw sanctuary.

As we left Everett, fine flakes swirled in the distance. Then a few miles farther up the road, by Marysville, the roads were wet. As cars drove by I could hear the comforting sound of rushing water. But traffic thinned out significantly as we approached Arlington, and the snow was starting to stick.

I slowed down and looked over at Jade. There wasn't any place to stop. I stayed in the slow lane and plowed ahead.

The snow was about an inch deep when I reached the exit for Highway 20 at the north end of Mount Vernon. I timed it right to get a green light and headed west. There were a couple more stoplights ahead, but we were the only ones on the road, so I rolled along without having to stop. There was only one set of tracks, but at least there was something. My next concern was the Swinomish Channel Bridge. A quick 75-foot rise.

In the distance, coming toward us in the east-bound lane, I could see yellow blinking lights. I thought, *A snowplow. Wish it was going our way*.

As it approached Best Road about a quarter mile ahead of us, it turned left to cross the median between the four-lane highway, then left again. *They're going to help us*, I thought, *We're going to be okay*. Still, it was dark, and I was tired. As we approached each intersection, I was afraid it was going to turn off, but it stayed ahead of us clearing a path.

When the plow reached the roundabout at the south end of Anacortes, it turned to the left, making the full circle to head east again. I felt terrible. I wanted to thank them, but there was no way that could have happened. I slowed, taking the gentle arc right onto Commercial. The snow on the road ahead of me was pristine, about two inches deep.

I had two more turns. I remembered what Randy had done years before. As I took the first, even though the back of the car fishtailed, I held on and straightened it out. The apartment complex was only about 500 feet farther. The sidewalk was slightly graded, so as we went up, I took my foot off the pedal, and we coasted into a parking spot. I thanked God for the snowplow and for having an apartment that was on level ground close to the edge of town.

### ~ CONFLICT OF INTEREST ~

Online, everyone was talking about email lists. Having one was now the *only* way to become a millionaire on the internet.

Of course, a woman in one of the spiritual groups was right there to help with a free webinar. I didn't care what her beliefs were. I attended her webinar because I wanted to learn about how to create lasting connections with the people who were responding positively to what I was sharing.

But after the woman led the group through some kind of mental exercise, I decided to ask a question. The woman responded quickly, and given her response, I felt like I needed to go to the library in search of a subject I couldn't even clearly define.

I felt sure I would recognize the concept when I saw it, but nothing in particular stood out.

Since I was at the library anyway, I picked up a collection of books that I thought might be worth reading. They included *The Secret: The Power* by Rhonda Byrne and *The Wisdom of the Enneagram: The Complete Guide to Psychological and Spiritual Growth for Nine Personality Types* by Don Richard Riso and Russ Hudson.

Maya had shared *Scripts People Live* by Claude Steiner with me. I felt compelled to drag it out of storage. To my surprise, the focus of the book revolved around one of the subjects frequently discussed in spiritual circles— the ego. In spiritual groups the primary goal was to overcome the ego, whereas during the events I'd been experiencing, my ego seemed to be irrelevant.

Steiner presented ideas based on Eric Berne's theory about the nature of communication, how people use language that can be driven by either The Child, The Parent, or The Adult states of the ego/consciousness. Steiner says those states can become scripts people use unwittingly to make life decisions, while also using them to try to influence other people. Like the way some people try to hold conversations in The Adult-based ego state to encourage people to become independent or the way some people use language from The Parent-based ego state to try to control others. This made so much sense when I thought about the influence of so-called "spiritual" gurus.

*The Wisdom of the Enneagram* reminded me that I could also search the internet, and I felt like I had been guided to information that needed to be known.

Unfortunately the information I found online revolved around a concept related to the Myers-Briggs Type Indicators, and when I posted comments about what I found in some of the spiritual groups, everyone dismissed it, completely, telling me that Myers-Briggs had been debunked so there wasn't anything relevant to my findings.

It took a while, but I finally found information that helped me understand their point. It was disheartening. All I could do was hope that someday I'd be able to find additional information that would help to support my discoveries.

~ ~ ~

The next time I visited the sanctuary, Jade was able to join me. Kiroc and Rocket had been moved to cages with birds of their own species. I couldn't find Rocket, but I was able to find Kiroc. Each time I visited I brought a few boxes of bananas, and Kiroc came to me when I called. While I stroked her toes, she ate more than I thought she could hold, then she climbed to the top and shut her eyes.

Jade took pictures of me, smiling, hoping that Kiroc's actions meant she felt safe, but as we walked away, my mood changed. I began to think about all of the other things that could have been going on. Maybe she was exhausted. Maybe she finally realized that Randy wasn't ever going to come. Maybe she couldn't take having to watch us leave again.

Jade and I went back to the car as I did my best to hold myself together. We drove up Highway 203 through Duvall, and Jade pointed out a bookstore. It seemed like a good place to take a breather after the stress of having to leave my friend.

I'd heard about Carl Jung, but hadn't read any of his work. I picked up *The Basic Writings of C.G. Jung* to see what it was about.

After scanning about 50 pages, which covered Freud, Oedipus, dreams, language, and aspects of the unconscious like instinct and will, I gave up. It wasn't what I was looking for.

## ~ S T .  L O U I S ~

In Amber's sophomore year, the Robotics team had grown to over fifty members. The coach split the students into two groups. Each team was going to build a robot, then they would compete with one another for the chance to go to the inter-school competitions.

Amber was chosen to lead one of the teams, but as they got close to the deadline, as each team acquired points for meeting standards like time limits to accomplish a task, Amber sounded frustrated. She said she heard that the calculations weren't being done accurately.

After the six weeks of build season, parents and friends were invited to an event on a Friday evening in the High School cafeteria where the coach was going to announce which robot had been chosen. When we arrived some of the team members stood by the open doors shouting greetings, but cool evening air dominated the space. Even though the cafeteria doors were just a few feet away, the sound of our steps in the vacant, tiled hallway rumbled low, making it feel more like a funeral march. Amber was a wreck.

Dread hit as we entered the cafeteria. I was never sure if anyone liked me. I was a single parent. Still divorced after ten years. I began to think one of the women was being friendly, only to hear, "So. What church do you belong to?"

Amber had to join her team members, so I was left alone. I scanned the crowd, and a couple to the left was kind enough to wave, but I walked by, knowing I wasn't welcome to join them. I didn't want to burden anyone with my presence. A couple of familiar faces emerged from the crowd. I didn't know them very well, so I left a number of empty seats between us so they didn't have to talk to me if they didn't want to.

Far to my left, at the end of the rows of tables, the robots were hidden under black tarps. Six weeks before, it made sense when the team decided to build two robots. It gave more kids an opportunity to be involved.

~ ~ ~

Now it was easy to see that Amber had been put in a no-win situation. I couldn't be angry about anything because Amber had been given the opportunity to lead one of the teams. For the same reason, I couldn't be angry that it was an older, all-male team that I felt sure was going to win. And I couldn't be angry for thinking that the other parents thought I was being greedy for wanting Amber to win, because I felt I was being greedy for wanting it, too.

Everyone knew she had two more shots at getting another position in team leadership. Jade made it to MIT. The other family's kids deserved a chance at those kinds of opportunities. While neither one of us said it openly, I was expecting Amber's team to lose. I felt pretty sure Amber was, too.

Amber appeared a few minutes later and sat next to me on one of the platter-shaped seats. She stared at the table. Her deep golden hair falling around the sides of her face. "They're going to use the other robot." She paused for a minute. "My build coach said mine is more robust, and he told me the other mentors agreed."

There weren't any tears. Throughout the build season and during the past week, Amber shared some of the problems she'd been experiencing, like the fact that the supplier for the arm she'd designed had run to the last minute, the constant issue they had with the weight limitations, and the fact that they had to test the robots in another school gymnasium, which was burning up time, but there wasn't any way for me to know everything.

Amber mentioned the rumors about incorrect data again. Her team members had been flying by me, and some of the parents were talking about it. She continued, "They got extra time at the trials yesterday. They've been duct-taping their robot together."

"Maybe you should talk to someone," I said as I watched the coach pull the tarps off of the robots, then grab a microphone.

"It doesn't matter anymore. The votes are in," Amber said. "The reason," which she put in air quotes, "everyone voted for the other robot is because it's lighter, more nimble."

The coach called the teams to the area where the robots were sitting. He approached Amber and asked her to demonstrate her robot's functionality. I caught the eye of one of adults who had been mentoring Amber's team. He was a mechanic. He knew what she'd done. He looked like he was ready to blow a gasket.

As soon as Amber finished her demonstration, the other team began. It was a bit hard to see, but after a couple of minutes, it looked like one of the parts had fallen off. From what Amber had shared, I realized that they were duct-taping it back together. Then they put it into a perpetual spin to demonstrate that it was light and quick, but it seemed like a useless parlor trick. The team hooted and hollered as the coach announced their win.

It felt ridiculous for me to be worrying about anything. All Amber had to do was hold on to her belief in herself, and she'd be chosen to be the build team leader in her junior or senior year.

"It's okay," I said. "The mentors have seen what you can do. You'll get another leadership position next year."

The team got a couple of lucky breaks and made it to Nationals in St. Louis. Amber wouldn't have to do much while she was there, but it gave her an opportunity to see other designs.

When I picked her up from the airport, she said she'd been up all night talking to a guy from one of the other teams. Neither one of them could sleep.

I said, "You stayed up all night?"

She said the guy wanted to hear everything about her path and Jade's. "He's from a team in Silver Creek. Their team is really small because it's an IB school. They don't even have a metal shop."

They followed each other on Facebook.

## ~LEADERSHIP IN ENGINEERING~

Once again Jade wasn't able to come home for the holidays. Then she told me she found a workshop that was helping to keep her busy. The students were put into teams and given specifications for a mechanical system. Each team had to decide if the system should be put into operation. There were three ethical issues associated with their final decision:

1) If they gave approval for the project to proceed and it failed, everyone in the imaginary company would get fired.

2) If they refused to approve the project, and it turned out to be a workable system, the manager would get fired.

3) If they gave approval for the project to proceed, and it was a success, everyone would get bonuses.

No one at Jade's table wanted to lead the team, so she took it on. She had been continuing her education in leadership at MIT through the Gordon Engineering Leadership Program.

After the teams spent a couple of weeks reviewing the data, Jade presented her team's findings. She refused to approve the project.

The project specifications were for the Space Shuttle Challenger.

~ ~ ~

One evening, as I was walking my usual loop, past the police station and middle school, then up the hill to circle around the playfields and elementary school, it seemed like something had shifted. I looked up with a different perspective—there seemed to be nothing between me and the stars. I was walking in outer space.

It made me acutely aware of gravity, the ability to lift our feet just enough from our planet that we can go wherever we want, but we're also held, just enough, so we don't fly away.

Jade had picked up *Stephen Hawking's Universe* when we were at the bookstore in Duvall, and I'd started reading it the night before.

I had also been working on a blog post where I was going to say my experiences were driving me to challenge everything I believe, then I thought, *I can't honestly say that. I believe in gravity and stuff like that.*

The next evening I picked up Hawking's book, and he described a concept which was developed by Einstein that challenges the current way we think about gravity called the "principle of equivalence." A gravitational field has a "relative existence...."[58]

I thought, *Okay, what I'm learning is challenging "everything" I think. Was that guidance? Synchronicity? Both? Neither?*

## ~ ASSISTANTS ~

All my life, I was led to believe I could trust science. I trusted that Galileo's version of gravity was true until Jade picked up Hawking's book. I trusted a lot of other people, too. Randy for years, then Kent. We made a verbal agreement about my pay rate, and I believed he would keep it. About a year after Kent and I started working together, he hired a sidekick to help with documentation. Another guy who had a passion for boating.

One afternoon when Kent and Sidekick were at my place reviewing one of our projects, Sidekick noticed that the clock in my room was different than the clock on my computer. He said to Kent, "I bet she starts charging you with this clock and ends with that one," clearly suggesting that I was cheating him. I was stunned. I didn't comment. As it was, Kent had been able to take advantage of my desperation and offer me a low rate until he paid off the guidebook project, which was supposed to happen after we finished version four, in the fall. I was looking forward to a pay increase.

After the Affordable Care Act went into effect, I waited for months, hoping I could go to the dentist I'd been seeing before the divorce, but I finally talked myself into going to the only dentist in town that took AppleHealth. The next best option was in Bellingham, and I didn't want to pay for fuel.

When I walked into the office, it was as nice as any I'd seen. I noticed a couple of young women standing near a door talking. I thought, *Surely, one of them will come get things started.* But neither one of them did. The dentist approached, sat down, and adjusted my chair. As he took one step after another, I realized that he was going to do the procedures alone. *That's weird*, I thought. *There's always been an assistant.*

A few minutes later he asked me to turn my head and said, "Looks like a filling fell out."

He got up, got some supplies, then he began to press silver amalgam into the cavity without even cleaning it. I thought, *I guess this is what dentistry is like for poor people.*

The dentist switched to the other side and repaired another cavity as I sputtered through water spraying all over my face, trying to act like it was normal, trying to be thankful I was finally getting some help.

~ ~ ~

The front door slammed. Amber dropped her backpack on the floor in her room with a thud and walked back to my bedroom office.

"The votes are in. I'm going to be the Program Manager's Assistant. Then the coach said none of the administrative positions will be hands-on." Amber's eyes rolled as she talked. I got up and followed her into the kitchen.

"I made blueberry muffins," I said as she opened the fridge.

"I don't understand. They saw what I did. They know Jade's at MIT."

I fumbled around, opening and closing cupboards, trying to help Amber figure out what to eat. We both knew what Jade had been going through.

"You don't have to say anything, Mom. I just thought this time was gonna be different."

I never dreamed one of my daughters would be at MIT, but the path Jade had taken to get there had been far from easy. I heard about one thing after another nearly every day. Being expected to do all of the administrative work. Signs in windows that said "No girls allowed," and worse. Constant harassment by one of the mentors.

I watched the team grow. I watched the coach and mentors as they created different structures. It was hard to tell what the true motivations were, if there were underlying prejudices. If Amber wasn't on the build team, she couldn't help with the design or build any of the parts. But it was still her junior year. She wouldn't like the administrative work, but I knew she'd do her best because she only had one more chance.

~ ~ ~

"It looks like you've been assaulted," Dr. Browne said, rolling his chair toward me.

"I went to a low-income clinic in May and the dentist told me I needed a couple of fillings. He didn't even clean the one on the left. He just packed amalgam into it. You can see that the damage is more severe around those areas. It isn't healing."

"I'll remove the amalgams and only charge you half my fee," Dr. Browne said as he stood up and adjusted his face mask. "We'll get them replaced immediately."

"Thank you," I said, as I tried to figure out how I was going to pay for even that much.

Dr. Browne prepared the equipment used to remove toxic substances and the hygienist adjusted the chair so I was in a reclining position. I closed my eyes. I thought I was finally going to get a break at the low-income clinic. Now I had to figure out how to deal with this.

~ ~ ~

At about 5:00 p.m. on Thanksgiving, I eased myself up onto the exam table, crinkling the paper liner.

The emergency room physician entered with his arms crossed and stopped about four feet away, not even close enough to clearly see my face. "What are you doing here?" he asked.

"It's been like this for months. I decided to try some Aloe Vera. Now my entire face is on fire."

"You need to see a dermatologist."

"My insurance won't cover it," I said as tears welled up. I hated getting emotional in public. Whenever I started to cry my nose turned red and my eyes got bloodshot.

The doctor walked out of the room. I saw a box of tissues on the counter and a mirror. I dried my eyes and wanted to hide. I looked like a zombie.

When the doctor came back, he handed me a slip of paper. "There's a clinic about 30 miles south of here. They might have better rates. There's nothing I can do."

I kept my eyes down as I thanked him and walked out.

When I got home, I told Amber what happened and added, "I don't have money for this right now."

"Can't you sue the guy who did it?"

"There's no way to prove it was the dental work. I'm going to have to ask Kent for extra money this month."

I had never been very good with money, but I began to notice that Kent didn't ever pay me more than a set monthly amount. If he owed me a lot of money after I'd worked on a project nights and weekends, he would extend the payments out month after month. I'd been managing, but I was still making payments on the bill to remove the mercury.

I called the clinic anyway the next morning and asked if I could make an appointment.

"We won't have any openings until mid-January."

"This isn't acne," I said, struggling to keep my voice in check. "I have holes in my face. The skin keeps peeling away. Can I please stop by and show someone?"

"Let me see what I can do."

She put me on hold as I wondered what was going to be left of my face by mid-January.

"Can you be here at 8:00 am tomorrow?"

"Yes. Thank you."

## ~ G O L D I L O C K S ~

When I got home from the clinic, it felt like I'd experienced a miracle. Within hours of using a steroid cream, my skin healed. I thought, *Thank God. I have a face again.* But within a day or so, the inflammation was back, and day after day, it got worse.

One afternoon when I was at the pharmacy, I mentioned it to the woman at the counter and she said she'd been using steroids for years. I hated taking medicine and wanted to figure out how to help my face heal. I'd been plagued with food issues since I was a child and wondered if something I was eating was contributing to the inflammation and dryness that had now spread up to my eyes and forehead.

It was almost time for bed, and I stared at a woman who looked like she'd aged forty years in six months. The skin around my eyes was pulled into deep wrinkles that I was afraid were going to be permanent. The directions on the steroid cream said to keep it away from my eyes, but I used a cotton swab to dab it as close as I could, under my eyebrows and in the deep curve along the edge of my nose as Amber called out from her bathroom, "Will you cut my hair?"

I looked at the clock on my computer and called back, "It's 10:30 p.m."

"I can't get a brush through it. And I don't want it to catch in the machines." Amber was still taking metal shop classes. She was determined to be Build Team Leader her senior year.

"Okay," I said. "I'll get my scissors."

Amber stood on a towel she'd thrown on the bathroom floor and pulled her hair out from underneath the one she'd wrapped around her shoulders. The ends glistened with gold she'd had since she was little. I'd never been able to figure out how to describe the color of the rest of her hair, but as I stood there, I realized it was the same as my new breakfast cereal. I'd switched from oats to rye, doing everything I could to try to stop the inflammation on my face, and the color matched perfectly.

"What do you want me to do?"

"Cut it off. Down to an inch or two."

I lifted one of the thick curls on the right side of her head and tried to hack through it. The scissors seemed to recoil, sliding away from her hair. I had to keep repositioning them and groaned, "It doesn't want me to cut it."

Long hair had been part of my identity since I'd been about 11 years old. I got a shag and people told me it was beautiful. From the time I was about Amber's age, on an almost daily basis, I cut it a little here and there to maintain the look I wanted.

One evening when Amber was about four, the sun was shining through the venetian blinds, and it fell across her long golden waves in diagonal stripes. She looked like a lioness in the grassland, and the moment seemed powerful. I thought she would always care for her hair like I did.

As I made my way around the back of her head, I said, "You know I've never cut hair like this before."

"If it doesn't look good, I'll go to a salon this weekend."

## ~ C O M I N G  U P  S H O R T ~

"Hi again, Nancy. Happy New Year. Kent didn't include the extra $300 in my December payment. Could you find out what happened?"

"Sure."

In addition to paying for doctor's bills, robotics build season had just started and parents brought snacks and meals to the team. I wasn't going to be the parent who didn't ever bring anything.

When I didn't hear back from Nancy after a couple of days, I sent a follow-up email to Kent.

A reply came that afternoon.

"I paid you extra in November. That's all I can do. Things are really tight."

I emailed back, "It's my money. I have doctor's bills."

"Your invoices are higher than I was expecting. Nancy will be calling you to review some of them."

"I did all of that work. I'm not adjusting anything."

I didn't hear from Kent for a couple of days, so I talked to a friend about how to handle the situation. She suggested setting up a contract for the new year, so I found a few online to use as models. I had a rough draft together when another email arrived from Kent.

"I've decided to work with someone else."

~ ~ ~

I couldn't believe it. I was completely out of work. Yet another man treating me like shit.

~ ~ ~

Still, it wasn't like I was looking into the jaws of death. It was an illusion. The fear that kept creeping up was my imagination.

Kent owed me a lot of money, and I was pretty sure he would pay it. I had some credit, and I was highly skilled. I just needed to start looking and something would work out. If I couldn't find something locally, there were a couple of nearby towns. Then I wondered, *What if he doesn't pay me? What if I can't find a job before my resources run out?*

I started to panic as I imagined what could happen.

I called Candice, a friend of Randy's that I hoped was still mine as well. She and her husband, Brian, let lots of people stay at their place. I knew someone was already living with them, but they also had a camper. It wasn't like I could even stay at their house since they had cats, but I thought maybe I could make the camper work long enough to get a job.

Candice sounded irritated. She said she couldn't make a decision without talking to Brian.

A couple of hours later, the phone rang. Pleasantries had vanished. She was the responsible adult telling the reckless child, once and for all, I was completely on my own.

"You can just walk down the street and get a job. There are plenty of places looking for workers, like McDonalds. You need to put food on the table and keep a roof over your head."

"I know," I said.

I didn't want to try to explain. It was too complicated. I'd overstepped my boundaries, and I was sure Brian was mad at me. I thanked Candice for her advice and hung up.

~ ~ ~

The Robotics Kick-off had started the weekend before, so Amber was staying at school every night working on production schedules. I picked her up at 10:00 p.m. and told her what happened.

When we got home, she curled up on the hide-a-bed couch my parents bought to use on Orcas, but never did. I sat on the dusty rose love seat that Tina had given us when her mother died. Practically everything I owned had been given to me by friends or relatives. I was so sure when I met Kent that he was going to keep our agreement. That I was finally going to be able to stop worrying. But maybe this was for the best. I had struggled for so long to make ends meet with my business. It was another opportunity to find a job with decent pay and benefits.

"I don't want to work at McDonalds," I said to Amber as she got up and grabbed an orange.

"I know," Amber said, tearing away a concave piece of the peeling and setting the bowl on the arm of the couch.

"I feel so stupid," I said, watching her pull off the stringy white fibers. "I don't have a website. My resume is out of date. I have a ton of work to do before I can even start looking. I'm pretty sure the money will come from Kent."

"Are you going to try to find a job in Seattle?"

"I'm going to have to try everything."

~ ~ ~

I revised my resume and applied to jobs in Anacortes, as well as from Bellingham to Tacoma.

I thought I could at least build a functional website in Dreamweaver, so I prepared artwork and developed the CSS. When it was nearly complete, I mentioned it to one of the mentors on the robotics team, and he mentioned Bootstrap. I'd forgotten that sites now had to be fluid, so they could be viewed on phones. I'd developed an obsolete piece of garbage.

Over three months had passed, and I'd only gotten one follow-up call.

I'd found a cozy little home in a corner of the world, a place that seemed so right at the time. Now everywhere I turned my skills fell short. Good paying jobs were few and far between in small tourist towns, and there was no way I could get through another year on minimum wage.

~ ~ ~

The robotics team made it to Nationals again. I told Amber we couldn't pay for the flight.

When I stopped by the school to pick her up one evening, the travel committee was making final arrangements, and they asked us about it. When I explained that I couldn't afford it, that it wasn't really necessary for Amber to go since she wasn't on the build team, they offered her a scholarship.

With the final local competitions over, meetings didn't run as late. But there were still things to do like prepare for fundraisers and give presentations to service groups.

One evening when I picked up Amber, she mentioned that some of the guys were talking about next year's leaders, but no one was talking about her.

"I hate to say this," I said as we pulled into the apartment parking lot. "But we may not even be here."

I opened the dented door and let Amber pass as I continued, "I don't know what we're going to do."

Kent was still paying me, but it was only going to last a couple more months. After Amber and I had dinner, I called Carolyn.

"I'm not getting any responses," I said to her after I explained that I'd sent out applications from Bellingham to Tacoma.

"Have you checked out low-income housing? Maybe you could at least get Amber through her senior year."

"I hadn't even thought about that. You're a godsend! Thank you!"

~ ~ ~

The next day I called the local housing authority and was directed to an apartment complex a couple of blocks away.

"Will anything be available in June or July?"

"I don't know, but why don't you stop by at 2:00 p.m. tomorrow and pick up an application?"

After the appointment it didn't seem like there were going to be any openings by the time Amber and I needed it. I thought, *We're halfway to June. Nothing is working.*

I called one of my sisters who was living in Arizona.

"You can come live with us, but I have company coming through July so you'd have to wait until they leave. And school starts August 3rd."

Arizona. Maybe it would be a fun.

A team member had given Amber a ride home that night, but once she was settled in her room, I mentioned the idea.

"You can't live in Arizona, Mom. No one wears black jeans there."

I laughed. She was right. I couldn't imagine wearing anything else.

"Most of my wardrobe is black, too. We'd look like aliens."

"We may not have any other choice."

"If I could go anywhere, it would be Layton High. You remember Jeremy? The guy I talked to on the trip back from St. Louis. I want to be on his team. It's small. Like when Jade started L2X3. I might be able to help build the robot. I still talk to him once in a while."

"There's no way that's going to happen. We might be able to make it to Everett or Renton, but we'll never be able to make it to Silver Creek. If I manage to find a job in the Metro area, we can visit. But I don't know if I should even be looking there. It's your senior year. I'm checking out low-income housing."

Amber replied, "I don't want to be here anymore."

~ ~ ~

I sat at my dining room table and reviewed a rental agreement that had come in the mail. The end date was May 31st, and it included a rent increase. Someone had purchased the property, and they wanted everyone to sign a new lease.

Amber didn't get out of school until mid-June. I couldn't sign another lease with my current financial situation. I sent an email to the landlord explaining that I wasn't going to be able to stay, but I couldn't move out by the end of May because Amber was still in school.

"We can extend it one month as long as you pay the increased rate."

I couldn't tell them what I really thought about leases and rent increases. I had to be polite and simply say, "Thank you."

193

## ~GOING, GOING~

Jade was graduating from MIT the first week of June. In December I'd purchased non-refundable tickets for the flight, but that meant I still had to cover hotel costs and food.

Candice and Brian were going. They were close to the girls, more so with Jade. It was humiliating. I'd asked them for help, now I was going to be spending money I shouldn't for Amber and I to go to Boston for the weekend.

I didn't know how anyone could think that, no matter how bad things got, a parent who helped their daughter get to MIT should have to miss the graduation ceremony, or that she would have to go through it without anyone attending from her immediate family. I had to tune out what anyone might be thinking about me. Amber and I were going.

~ ~ ~

We had to be out of the apartment three weeks after we got back from Boston, either to another apartment, which I couldn't see happening, or to Arizona, which meant we'd have to put what we could in storage. I didn't want to pay a moving company, but I didn't know anyone well enough to ask for help. I decided to see if Amber and I could do it ourselves.

That meant off-loading some of our furniture. I called Habitat for Humanity.

"Would you be able to pick up a bedroom set, a dining room table, and two couches in a couple of weeks?"

"Are they in good shape?"

"Yes. Oh yeah. One of them is really heavy. It's a hide-a-bed."

I tried not to think about all of the sleep-overs the girls had on it or what it was going to be like living without a couch as I called to get information on the sizes and pricing of storage units.

~ ~ ~

"Mom. If we move to Arizona, I'll be out-of-state. I won't be able to apply to college in the fall."

"Oh, my God. You'll lose the College Bound Scholarship."

I called Zola. She had a second home about 30 miles away. We met the next day so I could see if her place would work temporarily. I also mentioned Silver Creek. As I sat on one of her heavily worn floral couches she said, "If you want to move down there, you need to go drive around. See what kind of businesses are in the area."

I began to have difficulty breathing and realized Zola's place wasn't going to work. It practically killed me to get the words out. "I was hoping this would work, but something is affecting my allergies."

Zola nodded and said, "Lots of trees are blooming up the hill."

We hugged each other as I got up to leave. Even though it wasn't going to work, I thought I might be able to park on the property overnight and use the shower, but that would be a last resort.

I took Zola's advice and headed to the Metro area the next morning. I drove through run-down residential areas, up curvy narrow roadways, and through neighborhoods with deep green lawns and water views. I walked into a few shops, then found the Chamber of Commerce. They mentioned the community college, but when I got there, they said, "We only hire college students. Try WorkSource."

I walked into WorkSource, and they handed me the same packet of information I'd received when Amber and I tried to move five years before.

As I was driving home, Zola's suggestion helped me realize I didn't have to find a job that used all of my skills, and I didn't have to take a job that didn't use any. I could find a job that used some of them. When I got home, I opened up my search parameters and scanned everything.

I found an open position near Layton High that looked like a good fit, and I saw notices for a couple of retail jobs.

~ ~ ~

Amber and I went to the end-of-the-year social for the robotics team. I decided to tell one of the parents about my efforts to find a place to stay during July, and she said, "We've got lots of room. You can stay with us."

I thought, *Thank God. Problem solved.*

With a week to go, as I was loading boxes, the phone rang.

"Jason's mother died last night. Alicia and I have to fly to the East Coast. I'm sorry but Jason isn't comfortable having you guys stay at our house if we're not there."

I hung up the phone and switched gears. I started sorting out the clothes I'd need for a month and essentials. I knew one more person in the area I thought I could ask, but I didn't want to overstep my boundaries with her, so I had waited, hoping I could find something else. I sent Pauline an email asking if she knew anyone who had space for a month.

She offered the loft apartment perched above her garage that she used for business. She called it the Bird Nest.

I couldn't think of anything more perfect.

## ~90 DEGREES~

A couple of days later I got a call for an interview. It was the small business. I thought, *If I don't go right away, she won't think I'm very well prepared.*

"I'll be there tomorrow," I said.

I walked into the office and tried to imagine myself working there. It was nice. Kind of small, but the receptionist was well dressed.

The receptionist excused herself and came back with an application form.

*Damn*, I thought, *I didn't bring information to fill out an application. I thought it was just an interview.*

I decided to do the best I could, but within minutes I'd made a mistake. I crossed it out and felt sick. I tried to move forward and wondered why I was screwing up so badly. A few minutes later the guy who was doing the interview appeared. I felt like a kindergartener as I handed him the clipboard. He glanced at it and didn't even ask me to come to his office. He just stood in the entryway and asked me a couple of questions. I tried to act like everything was normal, then I thanked him for his time and made my way home.

~ ~ ~

The next weekend we moved everything into storage. I cleaned the apartment until it was spotless so I'd get every penny of the deposit.

The parents of one of Amber's friends offered her a room, so I dropped her off with her I-can't-believe-it's-come-to-this belongings. Then I drove to the Bird's Nest.

I hauled my suitcase, a couple of boxes of paperwork, my computer, and a cooler up the narrow wooden steps. Then I set up my computer on a coffee table that faced west, looking out across Rosario Strait to Lopez.

~ ~ ~

I had three weeks. I was sure we were moving to Arizona. Saturday, the 25th of July, we'd pack the car.

A couple of days later I got a call for an interview from one of the retail stores. I studied their website and practiced generic questions. When the interview was over, I felt like I had the job.

The next day, Amber and I drove around the area to look at apartments.

One of the property managers handed us a sheet of paper that said, "You'll need documented proof of an income three times the amount of the rent."

I said to Amber, "The retail store only guarantees 12 hours a week. They post additional hours on a job board. That isn't going to work."

The other retail store also contacted me. Again, the position was part time, but I scheduled an interview anyway.

~ ~ ~

I stared out the window through a frame of towering evergreens. Along the horizon, it appeared as if the earth was surrounded by glowing orange rings separated by dark and light gray bands speckled with orange particulate.

I kept taking steps forward, pushing on the edges of the world to keep it from crashing in on me. I set my alarm and hoped I could sleep.

When the alarm rang at 6:00 a.m., I wanted to stay in bed, but I thought, *I need to have enough consideration to show up for the person.* I practiced my interview questions on the trip south, but got tired of it and turned on the radio. I hardly ever listened to music. I hated getting songs stuck in my head. I scanned the news stations until I found the Spiritual Transformation station. As I turned off the freeway onto a six-lane surface road, a woman started talking about white butterflies. She said they were a sign that a loved one was nearby. I turned the radio off, then back on, deciding to hear her out, but she didn't have anything more to add.

I wound my way past a shopping mall to a large satellite shopping area. The store was on the right. I pulled into the parking lot and backed into a spot. The building was huge. The colors of desert sand. I felt like I was wasting everyone's time, but I got out of the car, managed to introduce myself to the sales person by the door, then dutifully followed the Store Manager to his office. I was less prepared than I had been for the previous interview, so I was afraid I wasn't answering the questions well when the store manager said, "Are you looking for full-time or part-time?"

"Full-time," I said without flinching.

"Okay. I'll let you know."

It was rush hour and nearly 90°F when I left. I pulled into a grocery store parking lot and sat in the shade trying to imagine driving to Arizona. My phone rang. One of the department managers asked if I could come in for an interview on Wednesday, July 8th.

## ~ WHITE BUTTERFLIES ~

I prepared for the interview and scanned Google Maps to see if I could find some rental options.

At least every other day, I went for a walk. The neighborhood was like a campground in some areas and a state park in others. Houses were adorned with wind vanes and boat decorations. One area had a roadside sculpture of miniature ocean-side homes, complete with a seagull on a post and a dinghy tied to the dock.

Two perpendicular roads created the small shoreline community: one that followed the shoreline and the another that cut up the hillside behind it. The shoreline road sloped up dramatically past the "T," so I usually turned there. At the top of the hill, I found a geodesic dome and marked it as my turn-around spot. I couldn't see any houses beyond that point, and I didn't like walking in areas where I was completely alone.

On Sunday it felt like someone had turned my anxiety up a notch. I was having difficulty making what should have been simple decisions. I went back and forth trying to decide if I should take the time to walk, then I couldn't decide if I should take out the garbage first.

The garbage won. I ran it down to the can on the side of the house, tossing the compost on the ground behind me and covering it with dirt and leaves.

For the first half of the walk, towering evergreens and drainage ditches along the sides of the road made it feel damp and cool. But when I turned right on the road that T'd, most of the trees around the houses had been cleared, so the sun was directly above me.

When I reached the geodesic dome, everything was quiet. I plodded back down the hill and turned left. After a car passed by, I crossed to the shoreline side.

I noticed a couple of white butterflies, then I passed a few more houses where I noticed a butterfly in the middle of the road. I assumed it was dead, but a few seconds later, another butterfly began to hover above it, then drop down toward the asphalt.

I was stunned. I pulled out my phone and took a picture as the second butterfly flew up and down like it was trying to revive the "dead" one. I tried to turn on video, but seconds later, they were in the air, swirling around me. I managed to get a shot of them together before they flew into the trees and out of view.

I had no idea butterflies had that level of consciousness. I walked back thinking about the fact I would have missed it if I had gone on my walk before I took out the garbage.

It was a surreal metaphor for what I'd experienced getting here. I was practically road-kill when Pauline helped me get the ground back under my feet and led me up into the same trees.

## ~ Q U A L I F Y I N G ~

I was offered the job, but the department manager apologized saying I couldn't start until the following week. I thought, *It's fine. I've got to find a place to live.*

~ ~ ~

Neither Amber nor I were happy that the road to the place Amber was staying was closing at 7:00 p.m. for construction for a few days. It meant she had to spend a couple of evenings with me. I didn't want to inconvenience Pauline any more than I had to, and Amber didn't have anything to do there.

I did an online search to find the Silver Lake school district boundaries and traced the map on a sheet of paper. As Amber and I prioritized apartments in the area by price, Amber said, "I just remembered Layton is IB, not AP. I'm not sure if I can even go."

*Oh, my God,* I thought as my mind seemed to burst into a million little pieces, then coalesced around the realization that she *had* to be here to help with this.

"We can check the website," she added.

We found the page about the IB program but couldn't find information that explained whether or not Amber could attend. As I scrolled down the page, I noticed an email address for the program director. I sent a note explaining the situation, but it was the middle of summer. It felt like I was putting a note in a bottle and tossing it into the ocean.

~ ~ ~

I opened my email first thing the next morning, and called out to Amber, "We got a reply!"

The director said it would be difficult because IB was a two-year program and Amber was a senior. Then he mentioned that there was community college about twenty minutes away. She could go to Running Start.

I told Amber she had to go apartment hunting with me. I couldn't get enough done by myself given the amount of time I had left. We generated a list of about fifteen apartment complexes, but when we arrived, one after the other had higher prices than the listings on the internet. My estimated income wouldn't qualify for any of them.

I drove up one of the main arterials and found one possibility. They said it would take about two weeks to process the application, so I told them I'd be back the next day with the documents. We stopped at another one along the same road, but no one was around, so we headed to #13, turning right off the arterial, then left into the parking lot only to find a note on the manager's door.

Amber groaned, "Are we really going to wait forty-five minutes?"

An hour and a half later the manager arrived. Another couple was standing by the door so I quickly called out, asking if there were any one-bedroom units.

"Yes," she said, "We should have one by the 24th."

When we met with her, she said that the income I estimated would satisfy their requirements. We pulled out of the driveway and headed home on a side road, right past the community college.

~ ~ ~

I was back at the retail store processing paperwork on the 14th, and the department manager asked if I could start in three days.

In order to be able to work from the 17th to the 21st, I made reservations at a Motel 6.

On the 23rd, I signed the lease, then I drove back to the loft, packed my belongings, vacuumed, and cleaned.

At 2:00 p.m., Friday the 24th, I threw my luggage, computer, paperwork, and cooler into our new apartment and drove to work.

~ ~ ~

We registered Amber at Layton High, and she signed up for their robotics team. We were ecstatic, of course, and thought that was it.

~ ~ ~

After we finished with the Running Start paperwork, we toured the college campus. I looked up a flight of stairs and saw some unmarked doors. "Let's see what that's all about," I said.

Amber countered my bubbly interest, which I often express whenever I find something new with, "Okay. I guess."

"What do you guys do?" I asked the two students standing behind the desk.

"We're members of the student leadership team."

"Amber's a math whiz," I said, aware that Amber was giving me the side eye.

"If you're good at math," the young woman said, "you can get a job at the Tutoring Center."

As soon as we were out of view, we were laughing, screaming, in complete disbelief about the impossibility of the circumstances, knowing how amazing that would look on her college application. Within a month, Amber was tutoring Calculus and English, and a short time later, French.

~ ~ ~

Somehow, in April, Amber "knew" where she needed to be. Somehow, a year ago in the spring, she and a kid on the team at Layton High stayed up all night talking.

It was as if someone was helping us build a kind of invisible machine or conveyance as I tried to work in piece after piece. One didn't fit. Another didn't either. Then I'd try one more, and it would be a small step forward. Slowly each piece created the framework that propelled us toward Amber's vision.

## ~ T H E  T A N K ~

I still didn't know how "right" the move was going to be for Amber. Over the next couple of months, it was like watching fireworks.

"Mom. Team A4R2 just made me the Lead Mechanical Engineer! I'm not sure how we're even going to build a robot with the equipment they've got, but they said we could get a new table saw. I'm going to go help them pick it out."

"If you can build a robot that moves, I'll be proud of you."

~ ~ ~

The mentors weren't sure what to think of Amber, a tiny young woman no one had ever met, but she held her ground, made tough decisions, and showed them what she could do with a table saw.

With the size of the team, she knew they wouldn't be able to build all of the features, but she knew the majority of the other teams would. She decided the most her team could do to help the three-team alliances during matches would be to focus on defense, the ability to block the opposing alliance's robots from getting close enough to score.

Amber ordered continuous treads and proceeded to build a tank.

~ ~ ~

"No one wanted to drive the robot at the first match, so I guess I'm doing that, too."

"Are you kidding? How did it go?"

"I'm getting the hang of it. It's pretty nerve-wracking, but Kim and Naoki are great coaches. And Will's a great spotter since he's so tall. It was like having a second set of eyes, since it's hard to see over the obstacles."

~ ~ ~

I didn't think I needed to take the day off to join Amber for the final matches in Mount Vernon. The team had been doing well in local matches, but they were going to be facing the top teams in the area.

My phone rang, so I stepped into the back worried there might be an emergency.

"Mom, we just beat L2X3 at the Northshore competition! We're going to Regionals in Portland!"

I couldn't believe it.

In the final match, an alliance chose Amber's robot to compete with them, and they beat the alliance that had chosen her old team.

## ~ R E D   R O W S ~

Almost as if on cue, as everything appeared to be settling down for Amber, an internet friend shared a link to a four-week course by The Centre for Applied Jungian Studies called the "Seeker's Guide to Wholeness."

I decided I deserved a birthday present--an exploration into my personal archetypes. An opportunity to do something really different.

It took about an hour to listen to the weekly podcast and write up notes about my experiences. At the end of each week, everyone taking the course had access to a forum to talk about them.

The second week, I listened to the podcast in the morning thinking I would finish my notes when I got home from work.

A few hours later I was out on the sales floor, and I saw a gorgeous baby carriage with black trim and three-dimensional red satin rosettes. I asked the woman where she got it even though I didn't know if I would ever buy one. Mid-day, as I was helping a customer check out, she put a pair of Converse on the counter. They were black with red roses on the tongues. The girls loved Converse so I wanted to take a picture, but there wasn't any way I could sneak out my phone. After work, I took an alternate route home, visiting with a friend along the Edmonds waterfront, then stopping by the post office.

There was a box covered with red roses in locker #623, my favorite number. Jade had sent a high school graduation package to Amber.

~ ~ ~

I posted a quick story on Facebook about the synchronicity of the series of "rose" events I'd experienced that day, then I spent a little more time on my notes about the "Seeker's Guide" podcast.

Shortly before I went to bed, I checked Facebook one more time. The first post featured Jim Nabors, a man I had grown up knowing as Gomer, singing one of my all-time favorite songs, *The Impossible Dream.*

That morning, in an answer to one of the questions related to the podcast, I had written about the only other Gomer I'd ever known. The name of the woman in *The Source* that connected with God in the well and later spoke for God.

Then I noticed that the orchestra behind Jim Nabors was aligned in red "rows."

I started crying.

I had been seeing red roses all day. Nabors, who was singing as the character Gomer, was now standing in front of red "rows."

The red rose.

The most recognizable symbol of love. It felt like I had received hundreds of them that day.

~ ~ ~

I finished packing my lunch as Amber ran into the kitchen.

"Mom! I just got another engineering scholarship! I've got enough to cover everything for four years!"

I stood there shaking my head, but smiling as Amber gave me a quick hug, then turned around and ran back to her room, her hair freshly dyed, now dark, like Jade's and mine.

~ ~ ~

No matter what, I wouldn't ever forget Amber's goldilocks. Somehow the universe didn't seem to want me to, either, or it was just the weird way my mind worked. But it turned out I wasn't alone. Apparently lots of people recognize the "Goldilocks' Principle." Three of them appeared during our move:

*One revolved around trying to find a place to stay for the month of July while I looked for work:*

The first place didn't work out because the woman's mother-in-law had passed away. Then the second offer, staying at Zola's place, didn't work. But the third option, the Bird's Nest, was more than just right. I got to see the incredible level of consciousness exhibited by the white butterfly.

*The second one involved the robots:*

In Amber's sophomore year, she didn't think it was right to choose the "nimble" robot over her robust one. In her junior year, Amber didn't think it was right for the team to put her in an administrative position. Being able to make the move gave Amber exactly what she wanted: the ability to get hands-on leadership positions on a small team.

*The third one revolved around trying to find a job:*

When I went to the first interview, I couldn't understand why I was making such a mess of things. The second one was 10 miles north of the school Amber wanted to attend, and it didn't offer enough hours. But the third job was just right in a way that I could never have imagined. The store was called The Rack.

~ ~ ~

I couldn't help but think about the wilted bouquet and the note signed, R.A.K. How I felt it was left for me.

At that time, I pronounced it rock, given the event I experienced with the fossil, but with the unusual spelling, the "a" could be pronounced either way. R.A.K. = Rock or Rack. As crazy as it seemed, it appeared to be both.

~ ~ ~

Full time didn't turn out to be full time. I was getting anywhere from 28- to 35-hours, and I still didn't have healthcare. As I cleaned up jewelry racks, loaded new merchandise on the shelves, and hung hundreds of bras, I tried to imagine moving into one of the management positions. I noticed that some of the managers were more active on the floor than others.

One woman was highly skilled in three-dimensional thinking. She was a master at reorganizing spaces to add more merchandise in ways I could only see after she was finished. Other managers goofed off with their teams. Every time I tried that with anyone in the store, I felt like I'd crossed a line that was going to get me fired.

One afternoon I heard there was a full-time position for a Service Ambassador in the Asset Protection department. The position was different from being an agent who was responsible for apprehending shoplifters. They wanted the employee to be strong in customer service. It was full-time, and it required computer skills as well as the ability to pay close attention to details. Even though the guy who had been doing it was nearly twice my size, I decided to ask him about it, and he told me to apply. Then one of the floor managers offered encouragement.

About a week later, I heard they'd hired someone else.

~ ~ ~

Late one afternoon, the Asset Protection manager passed me in the common area and asked if I was closing. When he approached the floor team that evening, he told us the applicant for the position of Service Ambassador hadn't passed one of the tests, so the position was open again. He told me applicants would have to reapply. I got it done that night and for the first time since I'd started my business, I had a full-time job with benefits.

~ THE POLICE ~

Standing at my post one afternoon, I looked to the right and saw the police.

The band's name was printed in huge capital letters on a tank top that was hanging out of place on one of the women's clothing displays. The rock band, The Police, released the song, "Synchronicity," in the 80s, but somehow at that time of my life, I missed the message. For a couple of days, I had been thinking constantly about the concept of synchronicity, which included thinking about the song, because it occasionally played on the store's sound track.

I wanted to take a picture of the shirt to document the place I saw it, its orientation to my post, but my first break was almost two hours away and it was short. My next opportunity would be at lunch, but I knew how strange it would look for me to walk in the front door, take a shot, and walk out. I stood there immobilized, glancing back and forth from the incoming customers to the shirt, counting the seconds like a Kit-Cat clock, trying to figure out what to do.

A few minutes later, it was gone. The large block letters and brightly colored swashes were hard to miss, so I wasn't surprised that a salesperson from the women's department noticed it. I thought about trying to find it on my next day off, but since I was planning to go shopping with Amber over Thanksgiving break, I figured I'd look for it then.

As Amber and I walked through the store a little over a week later, I said, "I want to see if I can find it." She laughed, flashing her kaleidoscope eyes at me as we walked toward the clearance racks. I thought, *It seems strange enough that one person would be thinking about buying a tank top with The Police logo on it in November, so there couldn't possibly be two.*

I rifled through the Small section, then sorted through the Mediums as Amber toyed with her new two-tone undercut. I started to feel like giving up, then, a few minutes later, I found it. I held it up so Amber could see, saying, "Guess I'm going to buy it."

A couple of days later, I realized that buying it was the only way I could document at least some aspects of the experience. I had proof that I worked at the store and the tag proved that the shirt was purchased there, but there was another, deeper level to it.

Before I noticed the shirt that day, I hadn't thought about the fact that I was actually employed as the "police" for the store. My job, among other things, was to maintain safety and security for the employees and customers.

There were significant, recognizable connections between who and where I was at that moment, the band's name, and the title of their most successful album.

~ ~ ~

The game always seemed to be changing in the social media arena. The latest and greatest way, we were told, to build our ever-expanding email lists, which every publisher now required, was to offer something for free. It was actually more like a trade. People got free content in exchange for it.

In 2014, I realized that I had something that would work. I had "receipts" that corresponded to some of the events I'd been experiencing. Book publication dates, photos, and screenshots of conversations.

I put together a collection of essays in a mini-book called *Synchronicity, Documented* and offered it free on my blog.

~ ~ ~

They lied. People still had to be convinced they needed the free stuff. And I started to think that they had to be convinced the information would help them.

My stories didn't offer anything but a glimpse into a world you could only see if you were really paying attention. I didn't have any methods I could offer that would allow people to achieve peace, get healing from emotional issues, or feel like they had become one with the universe.

A short time later, I didn't care anymore. I had reconnected with Carl Jung's ideas via a couple of Facebook groups, and I found this:

# I DO NOT BELIEVE, I KNOW

I said, "I do not need to believe in God; I know." Which does not mean: I do know a certain God (Zeus, Yahweh, Allah, the Trinitarian God, etc.) but rather: I do know that I am obviously confronted with a factor unknown in itself, which I call 'God.'

It is an apt name given to all of the overpowering emotions in my own psychical system subduing my conscious will and usurping control over myself. This is the name by which I designate all things which cross my path violently and recklessly, all things which upset my subjective views, plans, and intentions and change the course of my life for better or worse. In accordance with tradition, I call the power of fate in this positive as well as negative aspect, and inasmuch as its origin is beyond my control, "god," a "personal god," since my fate means very much myself, particularly when it approaches me in the form of conscience as a vox Dei, with which I can even converse and argue." ~ Carl Jung[59]

~ ~ ~

It was almost an exact description of what I had been experiencing.

# SPIRIT

IT WAS TIME FOR A CHANGE OF GUARD. My co-worker joined me at the door.

"It's quiet," I said. "I'm going to see if I need to complete any training."

I walked through the fragrance and jewelry departments just to make sure no one snuck in while my back was turned. Then I zigzagged through the Common Area, down the hall past the manager's offices, and around the corner that led to Asset Protection.

As soon as I stepped into the office, my phone rang. I looked at the area code: 509. Eastern Washington. My father had been in and out of the hospital for nearly six months after he and my mother had taken a fall.

I could hear crying in the background. One of my sisters told me that our father had passed. We talked for a couple of minutes, then I hung up, trying to figure out what to do.

I walked out to the floor and told my co-worker. My emotions began to erupt, but I managed to choke a few more words out, "I think I need to go home."

~ ~ ~

Was my father's spirit there? Had my co-worker and I been "informed"? The timing of my co-worker's arrival at the front door and mine, as I walked into the AP office, couldn't have been any better.

My father died November 1st. A couple of days later I saw a post about the Day of the Dead.

I remembered thinking I was happy he didn't pass on Halloween because I've never really liked the holiday. Especially the skeletons. I've always tried to avoid Day of the Dead celebrations for the same reason, but also because there wasn't any connection to my history. Our family was largely Celtic.

Then a friend shared a post about Samhain:

Día de los Difuntos/Day of the Dead descended from a Celtic celebration on the first of November called Samhain (pronounced Sah-Win), which celebrates this liminal time, when the boundary between this world and the Otherworld was believed to be more easily crossed.[60]

November 1st held new meaning for me.

~ ~ ~

Something similar happened with the passing of his brother. I was looking for information for my writing, trying to tie some dates together through photo albums, and I spent a few minutes reviewing a couple of paper collages that my uncle sent over the years of him, his kids, and his grandchildren.

My youngest sister called a couple of days later to tell me he had died. I took me a little while, but I called her back and asked again what day it was, what time. As I walked through everything I had done, even reviewing days I'd made certain phone calls, it seemed like I had been looking at photos of him that same day, near that same time.

~ ~ ~

For years, I struggled with the concept of "spirit."

I imagined that early on in the development of belief systems, someone thought they needed to come up with a term to separate the good and the bad in people, i.e. spirit was the good in us; the mind (or for some people, or the ego) was the source of all that's bad. As if they were separating the pristine, clear albumen of an egg from the yoke of human nature.

When I started hearing about "spirituality" and all of the methods people were using to help others "ascend" or become "more" spiritual, I thought, *How could the spirit become better? Why are so many non-believers good, kind people if they don't use any of those methods?*

I also couldn't figure out where people in the spiritual communities were getting their information.

## ~ C O N S E Q U E N T I A L ~

If I had been one of the first people on Earth, I imagine I would have wondered how I got here, in the same way I think most people do. If we look around the local landscape, there isn't anything that offers any indication. But I could imagine looking up, seeing a cluster of seven stars in the sky, the Pleiades, and thinking, *That looks like a community*. It wouldn't be hard to think, *Where else could we have come from?*

There are quite a few stories about the Pleiades:

In African folklore, the story revolves around a poor couple who feed a hen to a monk and her chicks follow the hen into the pot, so they were reborn as the seven stars.

In Australia, they're called the Seven Sisters.

In Japan, their name is Subaru, which means unite.

Dhyani Ywahoo said, "the Principal People, the Ani Yun Wiwa, originated in the star system known as the Pleiades, whence first arose the spark of the individuated mind."[61] She goes on to say:

"From the mysterious void came a sound, and the sound was light, and the light was will, intention to be, born of the emptiness: Creator Being, fundamental tone of universal song.... Compassionate wisdom arose as will perceived the unmanifest potential of mind streaming forth. Will and compassion together gave birth to the fire of building intelligence, and thus was formed the sacred triangle, from which all matter is derived, the Three in One. It is a mystery, we say."[62]

Three in one.

~ ~ ~

The Pleiades also appears in the *Bible*.

In the middle of the Aegean Sea about 200 miles east of Athens, there's the tiny Greek island, Patmos, that's not much larger than Moran State Park on Orcas Island.

In the year 95, (Apostle) John was sent there by the Roman Emperor Titus Flavius Domitianus. He says, "I...was on the island because of the word of God and the testimony of Jesus." He casually goes on to say, "I was in the spirit on the Lord's day...when I heard behind me a loud voice like a trumpet saying, 'Write in a book what you see....'"[63]

When he turns to see who is speaking, it's Jesus, holding the Pleiades.

~ ~ ~

That was never shared in any church I attended, so when I read about people originating from the Pleiades in *Voices of Our Ancestors*, it was as foreign as envisioning my unconscious as a dragon that could be enticed by the clear light of a crystal.[64]

When I read *Daughters of Copper Woman*, I could see the wild, craggy shoreline, where the pulse of life came wave after wave. I might have walked the same.

When I read the chapter in *The Source* about Gomer hearing the voice of God, I couldn't believe a woman stood in that place, but for some reason, Michener did.

Michener was raised as a Quaker.[65] Quakers were historically Protestant Christian, and they believe that:

- Everyone can experience the light within. They also insist on individual obedience to the inner light.

- They believe in continuing revelation: that God continuously reveals truth directly to individuals.

- Quakers reject the idea of priests, and ascribe to a priesthood of all believers.[66]

~ ~ ~

The authors of the *Bible* try to justify the authority of their God by saying "He" is "the God of Abraham, Isaac, and Jacob" as though that supersedes what everyone else believes.

I began to wonder if it was because they could say "the God of Abraham, Isaac, and Jacob" spoke to them, whereas the gods of fertility, storms, and the sky, which were often carved out of stone, "supposedly" couldn't.

Still, after thousands of pages of eight-point Times Roman text describing the fight to win the game of words about whose God is superior, after all of the laments, exhortations, and deaths, after Jesus "performed" miracles, people were still worshipping rocks.

In my 1989 copy of the *Bible*, along the side of the First Letter of Paul to the Corinthians, I had a post-it, with the word, idols, sticking out so I couldn't miss it. I opened it to that page and saw the sentence that had initially caught my attention, "Therefore, my dear friends, flee from the worship of idols."[67]

To make sure I understood everything in context, I typically went back a few paragraphs and I found this:

"I do not want you to be unaware, brothers and sisters, that our ancestors were all under the cloud, and all passed through the sea, and all were baptized by Moses in the cloud and in the sea"—never mind baptism didn't exist at that time… "and all ate the same spiritual food and drank the same spiritual drink. For they drank from the spiritual rock that followed them, and the rock was Christ."[68]

Paul had to be thinking, *Damn it! They won't stop worshipping rocks. Fine! Jesus is now a rock. I mean, the rock.*

~ ~ ~

Paul called Jesus a rock, a stone.
"(Jesus) sank beneath your wisdom like a stone."[69]

~ ~ ~

I couldn't help but think, if the "spirit of consciousness" or "God" can enter the "material" nature of a person, why couldn't God enter the material nature of a stone?

~ ~ ~

It's understandable why people are drawn to precious and semi-precious stones like crystals. But I was surprised to see how often crystals were used to describe the most holy things in John's "Revelation":

1) "...in front of the throne there is something like a sea of glass, like crystal."[70]

2) "...and the spirit...showed me the holy city of Jerusalem coming down out of heaven.... It has ...a radiance like a very rare jewel, like jasper, clear as crystal."[71]

3) "The wall is built of jasper, while the city is pure gold, clear as glass. The foundations of the wall of the city are adorned with every jewel; jasper, sapphire, agate, emerald, onyx, carnelian, chrysolite, beryl, topaz, chrysoprase, jacinth, amethyst...and the street is pure gold, transparent as glass."[72]

4) "Then the angel showed me the river of the water of life, bright as crystal...."[73]

~ ~ ~

Sadly we don't have to imagine what happened when Europeans came to North America hundreds of years later. We know that indigenous people's communities were destroyed because of their beliefs. But how many of us have heard that Europeans and Native Americans had completely different beliefs about some of the exact same things?

## ~ D A E M O N ~

My research occasionally took me on tangents. Writing is a creative process, and given the difficulty I've had with creativity over the course of my life, I sought help, only to find things circling back around. One of those instances occurred when I watched Amy Tan's Ted Talk: "Where Does Creativity Hide?"

She shared an illustration of a poodle claiming she knew she couldn't ever be an artist. All I could think was, *My drawing skills are still worse than that, does that mean I shouldn't be writing?*

She talked about the process that led her to write, *Saving Fish From Drowning*, a book about moral ambiguity. The idea started when she read an article about Iraq. Then she came across the story. She said once she identified the question, she got hints everywhere. She said, "Then I knew in a way that they had always been there…They'd been obvious, but they had not been."[74] She said it feels like you're getting all this help from the universe, but it may just be that now she had a focus.

My writing process didn't align with what she was saying, but then Tan said that sometimes it seemed like she knew things she wasn't supposed to know.[75]

She said there were things that were "quite uncanny" that would help her write her books.[76] During her research, she opened a book to a page that had the same exact setting and time period as her book, as well as a character who thought he was the son of God."[77]

Then Tan shared a story that she called a "chance encounter."

She had traveled to Burma and her friends drove to a place they hadn't been before. During a walk, she said something felt mysterious and ominous. A discomfort that she knew had to be the setting of her book.

In writing one of the scenes, "for some reason (she ) wrote about cairns—stacks of rocks—that a man was building," but didn't know exactly why.[78]

She got stuck in her writing, went for a walk, and came across a Chinese man who was stacking small and large rocks, round and fractured, often on an end point. She said she asked the man about them and that his reply was, "...exactly the meaning of my story at that point."

She said she has had "many instances like this."[79]

~ ~ ~

About a month later, I watched Elizabeth Gilbert's TED talk, "Your elusive creative genius."

She said that, "in ancient Greece and Rome, people didn't believe that creativity came from human beings. Creativity was a divine attendant spirit that came to human beings from some distant and unknowable source. The Greeks called these spirits of creativity 'daemons.'"[80]

Gilbert mentioned that Socrates believed he had one.

~ ~ ~

The Stanford Encyclopedia of Philosophy offered a little more information under the topic of Socrates's Strangeness:

"Socrates acknowledged a rather strange personal phenomenon, a *daimonion* or internal voice, that prohibited him from doing certain things. The implication that he was guided by something he regarded as divine or semi-divine was all the more reason for other Athenians to be suspicious of (him)."[81]

The authors, Debra Nails and S. Sara Monoson, suggest that Socrates' daimonion guided him on personal decisions, not on the development of information he was sharing with others.

~ ~ ~

One thing I began to recognize through many of the stories I heard, as well as through my experiences, was that the messages I received were only for me, or in some cases, for a couple of other people.

The specific information Amy Tan received certainly seemed to be just for her, but the general information she received was also important to me.

The message Amber received about leaving Anacortes and trying to move to Silver Creek turned out to benefit her immensely, me, not so much.

The message Jade gave me when she said she thought Nathan was supposed to have been her father appeared to be only for me, but since then, I have heard people talk about unusual childhood comments, so someone else might eventually find value in it..

Socrates recognized that messages he received were only for him. He refused to call himself a teacher.[82]

Jung didn't want anyone to create a Jungian "belief system."

~ ~ ~

Is this a central truth? The Creator/God doesn't give people information that should be used to tell other people what to do. What if everyone believed this was true?

If someone tells you they have received information from God and everyone is supposed to be following what God told them, you'd know right away it's not true.

## ~ M I N D S P A C E . 2 0 ~

About 25 years after the Beat Generation had come into existence, I felt like I had walked into a party where most of the guests had gone home. Of course a few people were still hanging around talking about the people who'd gone, so it felt like I'd missed something important. I wanted to hear what they had to say in their own words. I wanted to be part of their group.

Echoes continued to reverberate over time. I heard about the writing of Jack Kerouac and Ken Kesey in college. I heard about Allen Ginsberg, but the information wasn't as clear. He had been in New York performing his song, Capitol Air, with The Clash, and had appeared on David Letterman, sharing information about the 25th anniversary of the book, *On the Road* by Jack Kerouac. Eventually, I found out he was famous for a poem called "Howl." I wasn't interested in poetry, so I didn't follow up on it.

## ~ S T E P P I N G  S T O N E S ~

A link on Facebook led me to "Thinking Allowed: Conversations on the Leading Edge of Knowledge," then "New Thinking Allowed," the series of interviews hosted by Dr. Jeffrey Mishlove. They had been producing content for over 20 years.

One of the first interviews I watched was about Emanuel Swedenborg. Swedenborg was a man of science, but also regarded as a mystic. He lived prior to the events of the Boston Tea Party and the American Revolution. All I picked up from the video was that Swedenborg had a premonition about a fire in Stockholm when he was in Gothenburg. At that time, all information travelled by courier, and it was a two- to three-day journey between the two towns.

I found out later that Swedenborg had experienced a few other unusual events: another premonition about a fire at a mill, being able to provide information to the Queen of Prussia about her deceased brother, and being able to help a woman locate a lost document.

~ ~ ~

I watched video after video reveling in "Thinking Allowed" information downloads. People were describing their experiences in other ways: as the nature of our consciousness, the nature of the unconscious, and the Self. They seemed like better descriptions than "spirit." The events I had been experiencing were mental and verbal.

As I continued to search for people who had experienced events like I had, I found out one of them was Allen Ginsberg. In 1948, he experienced what he later referred to as his "Blake Vision." At first he thought it was the voice of God, then he felt that it was William "Blake himself reading *Ah! Sunflower, The Sick Rose*, and *The Little Girl Lost*. Ginsberg also described the voice as being "the ancient of days."[83]

~ ~ ~

Writers occasionally find gaps that they have to figure out how to cross. I had a big one. I thought, *How am I going to make the jump from Swedenborg (1688-1772) to Ginsberg (1926-1997)?*

I decided to find out more about Swedenborg so I watched Jeffrey Mishlove's conversation with Gary Lachman, "The Life and Ideas of Emanuel Swedenborg."

The gap disappeared.[84]

William Blake appeared in Allen Ginsberg's vision and William Blake had close contact with Swedenborg's ideas. Blake literally bridged them.

"Some scholars think that Blake came from a family of Swedenborgians. He and his wife Catherine attended the first General Conference of their New Jerusalem Church in 1789. The members of the Conference endorsed Swedenborg's statement that the things seen by the visionary "are not fictions but were really seen and heard in a state in which (he) was broad awake."[85] Like Blake, Swedenborgians had to defend themselves against charges of "enthusiasm" and madness. The Church that Blake visited was a development of the non-orthodox Theosophical Society which was established in 1783 by Robert Hindmarsh. Even though Blake eventually disagreed with Swedenborg, "a number of Blake's friends and fellow artists were Swedenborgians and met in the Theosophical Society."[86]

~ ~ ~

I continued to search for belief systems that would include the kind of events I was experiencing. I had reviewed a number of Pablo Sender's lectures on Theosophy which were sponsored by the Theosophical Society in America and had been carrying around the belief that it had significance to me.[87]

Helena Blavatsky, Henry Olcott, and William Quan Judge established the Theosophical Society in 1875, which Blavatsky insisted was not a religion.[88] The term was not new, originally it appeared in the works of early Church Fathers, as a synonym for theology.[89] It is derived from the Greek *theos* ("god(s)") and *sophia* ("wisdom").[90]

In *The Voice of the Silence*, Blavatsky says that within each individual human there is an eternal, divine facet, which she referred to as "the Master," the "uncreate," the "inner God," and the "higher self." She promoted the idea that uniting with this "higher self" results in wisdom.[91]

When H. P. Blavatsky began to publicize her writing, Charles Darwin had introduced the theory of evolution. While Blavatsky essentially agreed with the process of evolution, she says it starts with pure spirit, which descends lower and lower down into the form of matter. The complete process is defined as "emanation." She describes the development of the fetus like this:

"If it could be analyzed—by the microscope or otherwise—of what ought we to expect to find it composed? Analogically, we should say, of a nucleus of inorganic matter, deposited from the circulation at the germinating point, and united with a deposit of organic matter. In other words, this infinitesimal nucleus of the future man is composed of the same elements as a stone—of the same elements as the Earth, which the man is destined to inhabit. Moses is cited by the Kabalists as authority for the remark that it required earth and water to make a living being, and thus it may be said that man first appears as a stone.

At the end of three or four weeks the ovum has assumed a plant-like appearance...the embryo hangs from the root of the umbilicus almost like the fruit from the bough. The stone has now become changed, by "metempsychosis," into a plant. Then the embryonic creature...develops into an animal-like fœtus—the shape of a tadpole—and, like an amphibious reptile, lives in water and develops from it...(it) has not yet become either human or immortal."[92]

The Theosophical axiom "A stone becomes a plant; a plant, a beast; a beast, a man; a man, a spirit; and the spirit, a god" refers to this gradual evolution...."[93]

~ ~ ~

A stone: the fossil.

A plant: a material used to make paper.

A beast: my companions, Kiroc and Rocket.

The same material aspects of the three transformative events I'd experienced.

~ ~ ~

From Ginsberg to Swedenborg to Theosophy. Three massive stepping stones spanning the aeons of time.

~ ~ ~

Still I couldn't adopt Theosophy's entire belief system. I decided early on that I would only speak from my experiences, and Blavatsky's beliefs included the Law of Cycles, which went beyond what I knew to be true.

## ~ I N D I V I D U A L I T Y ~

A Person.

A Spirit.

Roughly a year after I attended the writing conference and experienced the event at the Macaw Sanctuary, the San Diego Friends of Jung posted Edward Edinger's lecture, "Encounters with the Greater Personality."

I heard the words, a new holy name. I had to take a step backwards.

~ ~ ~

I was in a completely different state of mind when I got back to my hotel room after pitching *Brave New Girls*. I put the business cards in a safe place, and tried to settle down after the terror, excitement, and frustration of the day.

But there was a question that had been tagging along with me for a couple of weeks: What would it mean for me to publish under a pseudonym?

It had been hard enough to pitch my book to random people. What would family members and friends think? Even the titles— "Whorifying," "Men Are Getting Off Too Easy," "Explicitly Not for Girls," and "Fucking Bastards"— were challenging.

Amber was still traveling to Orcas to visit her father. I was still dealing with him over custody issues and expenses. The last thing I needed to do was to give Randy a reason to think he could take me back to court as an unfit parent.

I sat on the edge of the bed and asked myself, *Who is the most famous person in the world?*

*That's easy,* I thought, *Jesus Christ. J.C. Okay, I'll be C.J.*

I didn't worry about a last name. The decision was clear. I was going to publish under a pseudonym.

I had talked to a few people at the conference about websites. I wanted to get it done right.

Shortly after I got home, I worked on the graphics, wrote information for the "About Page," and set up the specifications I needed for the design, doing whatever I could to hold my costs down.

One afternoon as I was scanning the phone book trying to figure out a good last name, I remembered the name of someone I knew in school. Devine. I thought, *That's perfect.*

*Half devil = Dev*

*Half divine = ine.*

I wanted it to be memorable. I figured the more irreverent, the better.

~ ~ ~

It took nearly four more years for me to realize that the name reflected an aspect of human nature that Carl Jung studied for most of his life. My pseudonym represented individuation, wholeness, Jung's term for this connection to the Creator/God, the Greater Personality.

~ ~ ~

In his lecture, "Encounters with the Greater Personality," Edward Edinger, a psychiatrist who studied under one of Jung's students, Esther Harding, talked about individuation "as a long, drawn-out process of inner transformation and rebirth into another being. This other being is the other person in ourselves, that larger and greater personality maturing within us. It's the inner friend of the soul… into whom nature herself would like to change us."[94]

Edinger talked about it as an encounter between the ego and the greater personality represented as God, angel or superior being of some kind. He said there is a wound or suffering of the ego as a result of this encounter, and went on to say that, "In spite of the pain, the ego perseveres and endures the ordeal and persists in scrutinizing the experience in search of its meaning. As a consequence of this perseverance, there is a divine revelation by which the ego is rewarded with some insight into the transpersonal psyche."[95]

I heard the same thing from person after person in discussions about Jung, but there have been so many issues in my life, it was hard for me to see a direct connection to "a singular wound" that occurred before the event with the fossil. The crab "totem," if I am allowed to call it that, was related to a deep early wound, the loss of Aunt Bernice. But it seems more likely that the event was related to the near death of my Self in my relationship with Randy. It appeared in a form that brought immense comfort.

Edinger said, as I began to see early on, "Each individual who has this experience, has it uniquely."[96]

~ ~ ~

Edinger shares a number of examples of encountering what Jung identified as the Greater Personality, starting with Jacob's story in "Genesis."

Jacob had tricked his brother, Esau, out of his birthright. Then, many years later, Jacob had to come face to face with Esau, and he was afraid. On the night prior to the meeting, Jacob met the angel of Yahweh. They wrestled until daybreak, which caused the dislocation of Jacob's hip.

(The angel) said, "Let me go, for day is breaking."

Jacob said, "I will not let you go unless you bless me."

(The angel) said, "What is your name?"

"Jacob," he replied.

(The angel) said, "Your name shall no longer be Jacob, but Israel." And he blessed him there. Jacob renamed the place, Peniel, which means, "I have seen God face to face."[97]

Jacob received a blessing and a new name--his second or his collective identity.

Edinger briefly describes Arjuna's encounter with Krishna as a "dialogue between the grief-stricken man and personification of deity."[98]

Then he shares Paul's story. Paul describes himself as "a slave of Christ," saying "I live now not with my own life, but with the life of christ who lives in me." Edinger says, "This is one of the clearest statements of how it feels to encounter the greater personality."[99]

Edinger lists a few more examples:

- Moses's encounter with Al-Khadr

- Faust's encounter with Mephistopheles

- Captain Ahab's encounter with Moby Dick

- Nietzsche's encounter with Zarathustra

- Jung's encounter with Philemon

~ ~ ~

Edinger shares a couple of pertinent quotes from Jung:

"It was then that I ceased to belong to myself alone. Ceased to have the right to do so. From then on, my life belonged to the generality. It was then that I dedicated myself to the service of the psyche."[100]

Jung said, "Nietzsche had spoken naively and incautiously about… this secret. But I had noticed in time that this only leads to trouble. That was what I thought was his morbid misunderstanding, that he fearlessly and unsuspectingly let (his Greater Personality) loose upon the world. He was moved by his childish hope of finding people who would be able to share his ecstasies and could grasp his transvaluation of all values. He did not understand himself when he fell headfirst into the unutterable mystery and wanted to sing his praises to the dull, God-forsaken masses. That was the reason for the bombastic language, the piling up of metaphors, the hymn-like raptures all a vain attempt to catch the ear of a world, which had sold its soul for a mass of disconnected facts, and he fell into depths far beyond himself."[101]

~ ~ ~

Edinger relayed a story that helps us understand the difficulty Nietzsche faced in the 19th century during the "new age of reason":

"Of all the books in the *Bible,* '1Samuel,' especially in the opening passages made the profoundest impression on me. In a way it may be responsible for an important spiritual element in my life. It is where the lord three times wakes the infant prophet in his sleep, and Samuel three times mistakes the heavenly voice for the voice of Eli, asleep near him in the temple. Convinced after the third time that his prodigy is being called to higher services than those available to him in the house of sacrifices, Eli proceeds to instruct him in the ways of prophecy. I had no Eli."[102]

Edinger says that Nietzsche was a creative genius that produced *Thus Spoke Zarathustra* out of absolute necessity, that it filled him with a particular sense of destiny.

Nietzsche says: "Has anyone at the end of the 19th century a clear idea of what poets of strong ages have called inspiration? If not, I will describe it.

If one had the slightest residue of superstition left in one's system one could hardly reject altogether the idea that one is merely incarnation, merely a mouthpiece, merely a medium of overpowering forces, the concept of revelation, in the sense that suddenly an indescribable certainty and subtlety, something becomes visible, audible, something that shakes one to the last depths and throws one down. One hears, one does not seek, one accepts, one does not ask who gives, like lightening, a thought flashes up. A necessity, without hesitation regarding its form. I never had a choice.

A rapture whose tremendous tension occasionally discharges itself in a flood of tears. Now the pace quickens involuntarily, now it becomes slow. One is altogether beside oneself of the distinct consciousness of subtle shudders and of one's skin creeping down to one's toes. The depth of happiness, in which even when it's most painful and gloomy, does not seem something opposite, but rather conditional. Everything happens involuntarily in the highest degree, and you gain the feeling of freedom of absoluteness of power, of divinity.

Involuntariness of image and metaphor is the strangest of all. One no longer has any notion of what is an image or a metaphor. Everything offers itself as the nearest most obvious, simplest expression. Here all things come caressingly to your discourse and flatter you. They want to ride on your back, on every metaphor you ride to every truth.

Here, the words and the word shrines of all beings open up before you. Here all being wishes to become word. All becoming wishes to learn from you how to speak."[103]

~ ~ ~

I couldn't help but think of "John." The tricks of misinformation and confusion that John didn't seem to be aware of. He was led to believe there was only one.

Story compression, elements left unsaid, and time jumps caused Jesus's story to spin into a super-natural belief system about a super-man that no one was allowed to question.

Can you imagine being Jesus, growing up believing that you were the only one? The one and only one?

~ ~ ~

In 1938 Jung was invited to participate in a celebration of the twenty-fifth anniversary of the University of Calcutta, India. Jung was familiar with the culture's philosophy and religious history, and the trip offered him a break from his intensive study of alchemical philosophy. Still, he took the first volume of the book, *Theatrum Chemicum* (1602) and, in the course of the voyage, studied it from beginning to end. That allowed him to compare European thought to his direct experience with a "highly differentiated culture."[104] He spoke with a number of people, but avoided so-called "holy men" because he felt he "had to make do with his own truth."[105]

When he visited the stupas of Sanchi, where Buddha delivered his fire sermon, he said he was overcome by strong emotions similar to those that occur when he encounters something of significance of which he is still unconscious.[106] At one point, he watched the approach of a group of pilgrims. He said, "my mind and spirit were with them…the intensity of my emotion showed me that the hill of Sanchi meant something central to me. A new side of Buddhism was revealed to me there."[107]

"Christ, like Buddha," Jung said, "is an embodiment of the self, but in an altogether different sense. Both stood for an overcoming of the world: Buddha out of rational insight; Christ as a foredoomed sacrifice. In Christianity more is suffered, in Buddhism more is seen and done. Both paths are right, but in the Indian sense Buddha is the more complete human being. (Christ's) sacrifice happened to him like an act of destiny. Buddha lived out his life and died at an advanced age, whereas Christ's activity as Christ probably lasted no more than a year."[108]

"Historical trends led to the *imitatio Christi*, whereby the individual does not pursue his own destined road to wholeness, but attempts to imitate the way taken by Christ. Similarly in the East, historical trends led to a devout imitation of the Buddha."[109]

~ ~ ~

I chose my pseudonym at a time when I had a limited understanding of what it meant.

It's meaning was slowly revealed, like many events I'd experienced.

It mirrored another concept I'd heard of called "christ consciousness," but what has been more important to me is that when I say the name, Ceejae, I hear the name of a unique kind of bird, a sea bird or sea jay. It brings together the two aspects I love most about nature.

## ~DESTINATIONS~

Ongoing unusual appearances, or synchronicity, of my given name, my daughters' names, the names of friends and extended family have fascinated me since I was in college. For example, if my given name was Xyr:

- I had two college roommates in a row that had the name Xyr.
- My ex-husband's grandfather remarried. His second wife owned a

business on Xyr Street. I have a copy of the stationary.

- I only knew of one other girl in the town where I grew up that was named Xyr. She is now living in my childhood home.

- I met the father and mother of a young man Amber dated. His father had two sisters, and one of them had passed away shortly before I met him. Her name was Xyr. It was even more amazing that the father's other sister had the same name as Amber's middle name.

- The woman at the Macaw Sanctuary who was wearing the same shirt had the name, Xyr.

~ ~ ~

After I decided to use a pseudonym, I needed to create pseudonyms for everyone else.

When I chose the stone, Jade, for my oldest daughter's name, it felt deceptive. As though I was artificially adding another "rock" to the beginning of my story. But these stories continue to defy "rational" explanations.

~ ~ ~

Before Jade was born, Randy and I were driving home from a trip to see friends. I saw a name I liked. Randy said, "If you're going to use it, you need to find out what it means."

The origin of the name was directly related to my father's name.

My father's name origin is stone, so it turns out that the origin of my oldest daughter's birth name is actually stone.

~ ~ ~

Amber's real name was based on the real name of my great aunt, but I used a different spelling.

Randy said, "The way you've spelled it, everyone is going to pronounce it differently." He was right. When we made that change, I thought we had come up with a completely original name, but it appeared in a couple of breathtaking places.

For example, if I said Amber's real name was Zyr:

- The first Zyr we met was on Orcas Island at the hardware store.

- Then we met someone at a pet store with Zyr as a last name.

- I've met many young women in stores over the years, many with different spellings, but pronounced the same.

- When I worked at the Rack with a five-person Asset Protection team, one of the women hired was named Zyr. She left and another woman named Zyr was hired a short time later as part of the Customer Service Department. I couldn't believe I was hearing the name again in the employee services area.

- When Amber and I went shopping at another Rack about 10 miles away, we crossed paths with Zyr from the Asset Protection team.

- I saw one today (4.4.23) on Twitter (or what's left of it). I took a screenshot, but for personal reasons, I'm unable to share it widely.

~ ~ ~

I finally understood why I had to marry Randy.

~ ~ ~

I finally understood why my parents had given me my birth name, and why I'd always hated it.

When I told Amber about my pseudonym, she said, "What I like most is that it's gender neutral."

~ ~ ~

My favorite numbers, which correlate to the date of my birth, which correlates to my horoscope, as well as other striking number combinations, also appear in unusual, unpredictable fashions.

~ # ~

There are many other things that have happened. I suppose the world could use a few more books or at least a few more stories.

# NOTES

## CHAPTER ONE | THE STONE

Because of what I had been told, what I had experienced growing up, and the excavation I had seen on Sucia, I didn't know at that time that fossil collecting wasn't permitted. https://www.researchgate.net/publication/282882420_Sucia_Island_The_Geologic_Story, October 2015, George E. Mustoe, Western Washington University

1) Richardson, Ronald W. *Family Ties That Bind: A Self-Help Guide to Change through Family of Origin Therapy*. Self-Counsel Press, 1989, p. 4.
2) Ibid., p 10.
3) Smith, Joseph. *The Book of Mormon*. Pacific Publishing Studio, 2010, 1 Nephi 1:5.
4) Ibid., Alma 25:15.
5) Ibid., 1Nephi 18:25.
6) *Holy Bible*. Oxford University Press, 1989, 4 Maccabees 4.10.
7) Ibid., 2 Maccabees 6.2.
8) Ibid., 4 Maccabees 6.2 – 12.19.
9) Ibid., 4 Maccabees 18.6 – 18.10.
10) Ibid., 4 Maccabees 8.29.
11) Ibid., Matthew 1.6.
12) Ibid., Matthew 1.16.
13) Ibid., Matthew 2.9.
14) Ibid., Matthew 2.11, 2.13.
15) Ibid., Mark 1.28.
16) Ibid., Luke 1.42.
17) Ibid., Luke 1.48-55.
18) Ibid., John 1.1 – 1.9.

19) Ibid., John 1.18.
20) Ibid., Genesis 3.8.
21) Ibid., Genesis 4.17.
22) Ibid, Matthew, 28.18.
23) Ibid., Mark 1.24, 3.11.
24) Ibid., Mark 16.17 – 16.18.
25) Ibid., Luke 4.25.

CHAPTER TWO | THE PLANT

26) de Haan, Edward H F, et al. "Singularity and Consciousness: A Neuropsychological Contribution." *Journal of Neuropsychology*, U.S. National Library of Medicine, Mar. 2021, https://www.ncbi.nlm.nih.gov/pmc/articles/PMC8048575/.
27) Oliver, Mary. "Owls and Other Fantasies: The Loon at Oak-Head Pond." *Google Books*, Google, https://books.google.com/books?id=Adn8JFEl7u4C&pg=PT39&lpg=PT39&dq=The%2BLoon%2Bat%2BOak-Head%2BPond%2BMary%2BOliver&source=bl&ots=aLaVuwbPAI&sig=ACfU3U0cDg9rC8Cy8EAop66y_A8V03eDOQ&hl=en&sa=X&ved=2ahUKEwjUpvfztfP9AhXxIH0KHRTACvU4KBDoAXoECAMQAw#v=onepage&q=The%20Loon%20at%20Oak-Head%20Pond%20Mary%20Oliver&f=false.
28) Hogan, Linda. "The Hands." *The Gladdest Thing*, 24 Feb. 2013, https://gladdestthing.com/poems/the-hands.
29) Middelton-Moz, Jane. *Boiling Point: The High Cost of Unhealthy Anger to Individuals and Society*. Health Communications, 1999, p. 40.
30) Ibid., p. 178.
31) Staff, TeachThought. "What Is Maslow's Hierarchy of Needs?" *TeachThought*, 20 Apr. 2022, https://www.teachthought.com/learning/what-is-maslows-hierarchy-of-needs/.
32) *The Holy Bible: English Standard Version*. Crossway Bibles, 2005, John 5.27.
33) *Holy Bible*. Oxford University Press, 1989, Luke 12.46.
34) Ibid., Luke 12.49-51.
35) Ibid., Luke 19.26.
36) Ibid., John 1.29-34.
37) Ibid., John 1.41-49.
38) Ibid., John 4.26.
39) Ibid., John 8.12.
40) Ibid., John 6.57.

41) Ibid., John 6.63.

42) Ibid., John 7.8-10.

43) Ibid., John 7.39.

44) Ibid., John 8.42.

45) Ibid., John 8.36-58.

46) Ibid., John 10.7-30.

47) Ibid., John 13.2-4.

48) Ibid., John 13.31.

49) Ibid., John 15.14.

50) Ibid., John 16.33.

51) Ibid., John 21.25.

52) McCune, Bunny, and Deb Traunstein. *Girls to Women, Women to Girls*. Celestial Arts, 1998, p. 18.

53) Ywahoo, Dhyani, and Barbara Du Bois. *Voices of Our Ancestors: Cherokee Teachings from the Wisdom Fire*. Shambhala, 1987, p. 32.

54) Bolen, Jean Shinoda. *Goddesses in Everywoman*. Harper & Row, 1984, p. 122-126.

CHAPTER THREE | THE BEAST

55) McGrayne, Sharon Bertsch. *Nobel Prize Women in Science: Their Lives, Struggles, and Momentous Discoveries*. Joseph Henry Press, 2006, p. ix.

56) Ibid., p. 378.

57) Ibid.

58) Boslough, John. *Stephen Hawking's Universe: An Introduction to the Most Remarkable Scientist of Our Time*. Avon Books, 1989, p. 30.

59) Purrington, Author: Mr., et al. "Dr. Jung Clarifies Misunderstanding of BBC Broadcast of: 'I Don't Believe. I Know.'" *Carl Jung Depth Psychology*, 20 Oct. 2022, https://carljungdepthpsychologysite.blog/2020/06/03/dr-jung-said-i-dont-believe-i-know/#.ZCtGmfbMKUk.

60) "Samhain." *Wikipedia*, Wikimedia Foundation, 16 Mar. 2023, https://en.wikipedia.org/wiki/Samhain.

61) Ywahoo, Dhyani, and Barbara Du Bois. *Voices of Our Ancestors: Cherokee Teachings from the Wisdom Fire*. Shambhala, 1987, p. 9.

62) Ibid.

63) *The Holy Bible: English Standard Version*. Crossway Bibles, 2005, Revelation 1.9 - 20.

64) Ywahoo, Dhyani, and Barbara Du Bois. *Voices of Our Ancestors: Cherokee Teachings from the Wisdom Fire*. Shambhala, 1987, p. 16.

65) "James A. Michener." *Wikipedia*, Wikimedia Foundation, 27 Mar. 2023, https://en.wikipedia.org/wiki/James_A._Michener.

66) "Quakers." *Wikipedia*, Wikimedia Foundation, 13 Mar. 2023, https://en.wikipedia.org/wiki/Quakers.

67) *Holy Bible*. Oxford University Press, 1989, 1 Corinthians 10.14.

68) Ibid., 1 Corinthians 10.1-10.4.

69) "Suzanne (Leonard Cohen Song)." *Wikipedia*, Wikimedia Foundation, 17 Nov. 2022, https://en.wikipedia.org/wiki/Suzanne_(Leonard_Cohen_song).

70) *Holy Bible*. Oxford University Press, 1989, Revelations 4.6.

71) Ibid., 21.10-11

72) Ibid., 21.18-21

73) Ibid., 22.1

74) "Where Does Creativity Hide? | Amy Tan." *YouTube*, YouTube, 23 Apr. 2008, https://www.youtube.com/watch?v=8D0pwe4vaQo, 11:15-11:31.

75) Ibid., 14:10.

76) Ibid., 14.40.

77) Ibid., 15:07

78) Ibid., 16:14.

79) Ibid., 16:57

80) "Your Elusive Creative Genius - Elizabeth Gilbert." *YouTube*, YouTube, 22 Mar. 2013, https://www.youtube.com/watch?v=4HBJa279i8M, 5:40-6:50.

81) Nails, Debra, and S. Sara Monoson. "Socrates." *Stanford Encyclopedia of Philosophy*, Stanford University, 26 May 2022, https://plato.stanford.edu/entries/socrates/, (Plato, *Apology* 20e-22b).

82) Ibid., (Plato, *Apology* 33a-b).

83) "Allen Ginsberg." *Wikipedia*, Wikimedia Foundation, 4 Apr. 2023, https://en.wikipedia.org/wiki/Allen_Ginsberg.

84) "The Life and Ideas of Emanuel Swedenborg with Gary Lachman." *YouTube*, YouTube, 1 Feb. 2019, https://www.youtube.com/watch?v=XZxl9eXVjck, 55:25.

85) "Emanuel Swedenborg and William Blake by Miranda Miller." *The History Girls*, http://the-history-girls.blogspot.com/2019/06/emanuel-swedenborg-and-william-blake-by.html.

86) Ibid.

87) "Theosophy." *Living Theosophy*, 9 Aug. 2015, http://pablosender.com/%20theosophy/.

88) "Theosophy." *Wikipedia*, Wikimedia Foundation, 4 Apr. 2023, https://en.wikipedia.org/wiki/Theosophy.

89) *Faivre, Antoine (1994). Access to Western Esotericism. SUNY Series in Western Esoteric Traditions. Albany, NY: State University of New York Press, p. 24.*

90) *Ibid.*

91) "Theosophy." *Wikipedia*, Wikimedia Foundation, 4 Apr. 2023, https://en.wikipedia.org/wiki/Theosophy, "Personal Development and Reincarnation."

   *Campbell, Bruce F. (1980). Ancient Wisdom Revived: A History of the Theosophical Movement. Berkeley: University of California Press, p 54.*

92) "Evolution." *Evolution - Theosophy Wiki*, https://theosophy.wiki/en/Evolution, "Gradual evolution."

93) Ibid.

94) "Edward Edinger - Encounters with the Greater Personality." *YouTube*, YouTube, 13 Nov. 2013, https://www.youtube.com/watch?v=kAlCeJ4LuRk, 7:30.

95) Ibid., 13:00.

96) Ibid., 14:00.

97) Ibid., 19:45.

98) Ibid., 32:00.

99) Ibid., 44:30.

100) Ibid., 46:30.

101) Ibid., 52:35-53:50.

102) Ibid., 58:30.

103) Ibid., 1:04:30.

104) Jung, C. G., and Jaffé Aniela. *Memories, Dreams, Reflections.* Vintage Books, 1965, p. 275.

105) Ibid.

106) Ibid., p. 278.

107) Ibid., p. 279.

108) Ibid., p. 280.

109) Ibid.

# ACKNOWLEDGMENTS

MOST OF ALL, I THANK GOD for giving me this incredible life path. I never dreamed life could be like this.

I would like to thank the people in all of the writer's groups I've attended for their willingness to help as I learned the craft. This book is still far from perfect, but I have reached a point where I want to share the information instead of worrying about whether or not I have done it "right" by someone else's standards.

I would like to thank all of the people that have crossed my path, that have listened to early drafts of these stories, as well as my frustrations with the writing process, and offered their support.

There have been a couple of readers along the way, including my friend Rebecca, who hasn't read all of it, but still encouraged me. I hope you will understand that this is the story I had to tell.

Others include Pauline who supported me on a couple of occasions when I truly needed it. I can never thank you enough for letting me stay in the Bird's

Nest. I didn't share the story about the butterflies with you because I couldn't find the right words for the ending, and now it seems so simple.

R_B has also been there for me for many years. Without him I wouldn't have known who is living in my childhood home. I was able to take Amber on a tour after my father passed away, and I know she appreciated that immensely. I hope you know how much your friendship means to me.

I want to thank Aunt Bernice, who was so fully there for me.

I want to thank my parents. My father, for all of his support, especially when he shared a few experiences that enabled him to know God exists. And my mother for her suggestion about the sanctuary and directing us back to the house in Anacortes, without a word, of course.

I want to thank my daughters for allowing me to spend this time with them. Our life together has been more beautiful than I could have ever imagined. I love you to the ends of the universe.

I would also like to thank all of the writers throughout time who have had the courage to share the stories of their lives so the world can understand the breadth and depth of the nature of humanity.

Made in the USA
Columbia, SC
08 May 2024

34980928R00143